IN THE HELL OF AUSCHWITZ
THE WARTIME MEMOIRS OF JUDITH STERNBERG NEWMAN

To the memory of
MY FAMILY
all of whom, except my father,
lost their lives in Auschwitz;
and
to the memory of
all the other victims who perished there.

IN MEMORIAM

MY PARENTS
Ismar Sternberg
Regina Sternberg
MY SISTERS
Charlotte Preis, *nee* Sternberg, Age 25
Herta Sternberg, Age 22
MY BROTHERS
Sally Sternberg, Age 26
Siegfried Sternberg, Age 22
Artur Sternberg, Age 18
MY FIANCÉ
Dr. Martin Tallert
CHARLOTTE'S HUSBAND
Werner Preis
AND THEIR LITTLE DAUGHTER
Eva, Age 5
MY UNCLE AND AUNT
George Sternberg
Paula Sternberg

J. S. N.

TABLE OF CONTENTS

I

I WAS seventeen years old when my dear father died suddenly of a heart attack. At the time I thought the world was coming to an end for me.

My father's untimely death was a great tragedy for us all, and especially for my dear mother, who was now left alone with all her cares and worries — life under Hitler was very hard for us Jews.

Since 1933 my parents had known only fear and anxiety about what the future might bring. I was the third-oldest of the children. My oldest sister, Charlotte, was married, but there were still five of us left for my mother to provide for. My youngest brother was a boy of twelve when we lost our father. My sister Herta was at home with my mother, and two of my brothers were attending special courses at a trade school in Beuthen in Upper Silesia, which was to prepare them for their emigration to Palestine. It was 1937. I myself had just begun my training as a student nurse in a Breslau hospital. My mother had been forced to give up our business, the running of which had gradually been made more and more difficult by the Nazis, and the family was living on the income from our holdings. Not for very long, though, for the Nazis took everything away from us, and soon we were no longer in possession of our properties.

But this was not the worst by far, nor the most feared. Life was getting harder all the time. Pogroms of the Jewish people had started, and my mother trembled for the life of her sons. My older brothers were planning to emigrate to Palestine, and in 1938 all formalities for the journey had been completed; but at the last moment the thought of leaving their mother and the rest of the family behind in such difficult times made them return their tickets and passports in order to stay with us and await a time for joint departure. The only happiness that remained for us was the warmth and harmony of our closely knit family circle.

In 1939 I was given an opportunity to go to England as a student nurse, and my mother with heavy heart gave me her permission to accept this post. Yet I also could not bear the thought of leaving and perhaps never again seeing my mother, and so I let my papers lapse. I remained at the hospital, where I completed my studies and became a registered nurse.

In 1940 we received permission to enter Paraguay for the purpose of settling there. We made our preparations and were all ready to leave with our overseas trunks packed and ready to be sent to Bremen. When we received our passports, we sent to the consul in Bremen to get our visas. But fate turned against us once more. We were unable to obtain a transit visa, and there was nothing left for us to do but return to Breslau and there continue our troubled existence.

After the war broke out, our life became worse day by day. Little by little, all of our common rights were taken from us. We were made to leave our homes and live in a few small rooms. Radios, gold, silver, and other articles of value had to be handed over, as well as our clothes and furs. We no longer had any right to our savings accounts. We were told how much we were expected to spend for our living expenses. We were forbidden to use trolley cars and railroads.

Jews were selected to do the dirtiest and heaviest jobs. Bicycles had to be surrendered, and people had to walk to work, often several kilometers, even in the depth of winter. Jews were deprived of their ration cards for clothing, resulting in a lack of working clothes and comfortable shoes. We were forbidden to use parks and public walks; the park benches bore in white lettering the words: "Strictly off limits for Jews." Store signs proclaimed in large print: "Jews will not be served," or "Goods will not be sold to Jews." Meat, vegetables, fruit, fats, and other items were stricken off our food-ration cards. We were required to wear stars bearing the word "Jew" on our clothes and coats. We were not allowed to visit movie houses and theaters — in other words, our cemetery was our only place of relaxation and rest. Our synagogues had long since been burned down by the Nazis and party members, and religious services had to be held in makeshift quarters. Sometimes during the service stones were flung through the windows, usually hurled by members of the Hitler Youth Group. The door to our apartment had to be marked "Jew," so that we were helplessly exposed to thievery and pilfering. All women and men were forced to adopt the epithet of Sarah or Israel.

Every four weeks we were required to report to the Gestapo, and if someone forgot to mention the by-name, this was sufficient reason to dispatch him to one of the annihilation camps in Poland. When this happened, the usual procedure was to return the urn containing the victim's ashes to his Jewish community by parcel post, to be delivered upon payment of a certain sum. The cause of death, in most cases, was given as pneumonia, or stroke in the case of an older person. On every Jewish holiday there always were arrests and other pogroms. Nevertheless we suffered everything stoically, and we all believed it could not possibly get any worse. But still we were not left in peace.

The Jews were not the only ones persecuted by the Nazis. Nuns and monks were taken out of their cloisters, driven in trucks through the streets, and subjected to the mockery of the populace. Their habits were taken from them, and they were forced to work in factories. If they refused, they were put into concentration camps. Cloisters were shut down. Thus many ministers and priests were killed in the concentration camps because they would not yield to the Germans. Images of Jesus were removed from the churches and pictures of the Fuhrer were substituted. They said that Jesus could not have been any better than the rest of the Jews, and they refused to worship a Jew. They shouted: "Hitler is our God!" Confirmations and weddings were held in the name of the Fuhrer only. I remember that many people opposed this, but these poor unfortunates were simply disposed of. Parents no longer had any authority over their children; the Hitler groups were the educators. A parent, for instance, was not allowed to spank his child if he was wearing the uniform. Often a child caused his own father or mother to be sent to prison. Young girls were urged to have babies even though they were unmarried. They were told that not every girl could become a German wife, but all of them could be German mothers. The government paid a certain fee for each child, and the more children they had, the higher were the monetary rewards. Moral principles had sunk to a very low level, and young people knew no respect — neither for God nor for their parents. They were brought up to hate everyone who was not of Teutonic descent. And they were so sure of their song: "Germany Above All, Above All in the World." That was the reason why they possessed the audacity to inflict such unbelievable tortures on innocent people.

Soon emigration transports to Poland began. People had to leave home with but a small suitcase or a knapsack, mothers with their infants in their arms; they were entering a world of black fear. I remember it well. It was winter, and very cold. We were kept in a temporary camp in our home town, where people spent three to five days lying on the floor wrapped only in their blankets and unable to obtain warm food for their children. They asked: "What could possibly happen to us worse than this? We can only die." Death no longer held any terror, but first these martyrs were destined to suffer in a most horrible and gruesome way. Death would come later, in Poland, where the poor victims were made to dig their own graves. The digging completed, they were told to march past the ditches with their children, while the SS and other military units shot them — right into the open pits. Not all of them were fortunate enough to die at once, and some of them were buried alive. I was still working at my job in the hospital when I first heard about this from good friends, who advised us to commit suicide at home when our turn came rather than be sent away. They told us what they had seen with their own eyes, but we could not believe these stories until we had personally convinced ourselves of the cruelties of the Nazis.

Our destiny soon caught up with us. It was five o'clock in the morning on February 23, 1942, when an unusual commotion awakened me at the hospital, where, as *Stationsschwester* (nurse in charge of the children's ward), I had my lodgings. There was excited running back and forth in the corridors. I looked out the window and saw police threatening us with rifles. The gatekeeper and several physicians had already been picked up. Trembling all over, I began to pack my belongings. The policemen consoled us, saying not to worry, for we would merely be sent to a work camp. So great was our desire to live that we believed these criminals, though our hearts were heavy with grief. Oberschwester (Chief Nurse) Toni, however, was not to be fooled. She said: "You pigs shall not get me!" She went upstairs, took a large dose of cyanide, and when she came down dropped dead at their feet. I was informed that my name was not on the list, since I had been reclaimed by the hospital for a few more weeks, but when I learned that my mother and my whole family were included, I did not hesitate to volunteer to go along too. It was then that they took me to the temporary camp, where I was reunited with my mother, who had already been searching for me with great anxiety.

We rushed into each other's arms. "We'll accept our fate, whatever it may be — to live or die together." My mother, no longer caring for her own life, only prayed that her children might be spared. As a Jewish mother she bore her lot bravely, but her eyes betrayed her grief and suffering.

My heart ached when my mother told me how she had been forced out of her apartment that morning. She had not even had time to put on her coat, for she had been helping my brothers and sister get their things together to pack in a knapsack, without thinking of herself. The German barbarians could not wait any longer; a push with a rifle butt knocked her against the wall. Then she was told: "Hurry up and get out of here. You won't be needing your things any more." My mother left, and right then, while she was watching, the Gestapo put their seal on the apartment. At the last moment I was able to get a coat for my mother so that she was somewhat protected from the bitter cold.

I was engaged at the time, and we had been planning to be married in two weeks, on March 21. The rabbi gave us blessings in the transit camp, and we had a simple religious wedding ceremony. However, the marriage was not official because we were unable to get our papers for the civil ceremony, and so the religious ceremony was not valid according to the laws of the land. But my fiancé and I were now together, entering on this road of sorrow.

There were about fourteen hundred people in the temporary camp, three hundred of whom were children. They played unconcernedly, running here and there and building castles in the sand. But there was a mute scream for help written on the faces of the grownups, and fearful hesitation when their turn to join the transports came. During the second night alone there were eighty suicides in the camp. Eighty others were picked out to take their places in the transport. They were not cowards, afraid to live, but they did not want to have their lives taken by the Nazi murderers. Oh, how it must have grieved a mother to poison her own child, though she wanted only to give her little one an easier death, even at the cost of becoming a murderess. Then, when she saw her dead child sleeping so peacefully, she would poison herself. Many times people implored me, "Nurse, please, give me an injection to let me die. Oh, please, do me this favor…" But I would have no part in the murder of a fellow human being; I still believed things would turn out all right in the end. Just in case, though, I carried a sufficient quantity of drugs with me to take care of my own family, should it become necessary. Among my friends who committed suicide in this camp were the organist Berger and his wife, and when their son and their daughter, also a nurse, saw this, they also took cyanide.

It was two o'clock at night when loud shouting awakened us. "Get up!" SS men carrying long sticks were walking between the rows and striking the sleeping bodies, left and right. The Breslau Gestapo stood there, cynical smiles on their lips, and calmly distributed numbers. We were loaded into trolleys and taken to the freight depot. There, eighty of us, plus our baggage, were crammed into a stock car. One tiny barred window provided air for all. There were no sanitary facilities, and our car was sealed from the outside. It was oppressively hot within. We begged for water, but were told that we would get hot coffee as soon as we reached our destination. There was no food left for the infants, and mothers, despairing at the hunger cries of their babies, would have jumped out of the moving car if it had been possible.

It was Friday evening. We held our religious services. No light and no star shone for us; it was pitch-black all around us. Dr. Skaller, a physician from Breslau, led us in devotions. He tried to comfort us: "The Holy Book says that after we have celebrated the darkest of Sabbaths, then the light will begin to burn brightly for us again, and our liberation is near." At these words our hearts felt a little lighter again. Then our Zionist girls started to sing Hebrew songs. All of us joined in the "Hatikvah." The last song of the night was *"Ein Schiff fahrt heimwarts, in das Land seiner Ahnen, blauweisses Fahnlein flattert im Wind"* (A ship sails home, into the land of my ancestors, its blue-white flag fluttering in the wind). Our eyes became moist at this, for we did not know where we were going — perhaps to our heavenly home — and would we ever see Palestine again, the homeland of the Jews?

At the break of dawn, we were still a long way from our destination. The sky was blood red. Suddenly we heard Dr. Skaller's voice, singing softly and solemnly, *"Morgenrot, Morgenrot, leuchtest mir zum Fruhen Tod"* (Morning's red, morning's red, your glow tells me I'll soon be dead). It was so quiet that one could have heard a pin drop. We all bent our heads. The children were still asleep on their mothers' laps.

For one more entire day we were confined to this airless, dirty stock car. (Later we learned that another transport of about sixteen hundred people from Upper Silesia was added to our train *en route* to Auschwitz.) Some of us had saved a piece of bread from the camp. We were all very low in spirits, exhausted and despondent. My fiancé, Dr. Martin Tallert, whom I loved above everything, bade me farewell as if we were never to see each other again. I looked at him, my eyes filling with tears, a lump forming in my throat. I couldn't speak. When I had controlled myself, I told him, "You will, and you must, live; we'll see happy days again, once all this is over. We'll see your dear sisters in Palestine again too." Oh, how very much he wanted to live, if only to witness the downfall of Nazi Germany, in retaliation for our suffering. For this reason alone he was glad to bear anything.

The second day passed. As night approached, we drifted into sleep, leaning on one another. At 2 A.M. there was shouting outside. "Get out at once, you dogs!" There were no ladders by which to descend from the cars, so we had to jump down. The men among us helped us as much as they could, and some of them broke their legs in the jump. They were left lying on the ground to be beaten, for as soon as we touched ground, hundreds of SS men with long cudgels hit us indiscriminately. The sick were calling for help, and they were told: "Soon you'll get to the hospital; there you'll be better off, you pigs." When our baggage was unloaded, they shouted: "Everything remains on the ground; you'll get your things back in the camp." Those who tried to salvage their most precious possessions received blows on their backs that knocked them down. They beat us so violently that families were unable to stay together, and lost track of one another without even having had a chance to say good-by. The men were separated from the women and children and lined up on one side. The sky was black. In the distance we saw barbed-wire fences with hundreds of lights. Then we knew: it was to be the concentration camp for us. We could hear terrible cries for help and the sound of beatings. Not even the smallest children were safe from the cudgel. Mothers had to wrap their infants in blankets, and when they had several children to carry, and one of them fell down, she and the child were both beaten as punishment. I tried to get one last glimpse of my three brothers, but in vain.

Soon several large trucks appeared. Young girls, women, children, the sick, and the elderly were thrown onto the trucks by the SS barbarians. The truck was overloaded to such a degree that the people at the bottom were trampled and suffocated by the ones piled on top. Mothers were calling for their children; children cried for their mothers. It was a sight I shall not forget as long as I live. From among eight hundred women, they selected 198 of us, and we had to line up separately. I belonged to this group. They told us that we would be reunited with the others once we were in camp. Suddenly I saw, in a long row lined up on the other side, my dear mother. She looked at me with wet eyes, and her last words were "Take care of your sister." Her eyes followed me to the last. Firmly rejecting all negative thoughts, I called to her, "Mommy, we'll see each other in camp."

We 198 women were counted off exactly. An officer asked us whether we were all healthy, for the sick could ride on the truck. Then we proceeded, under guard, to march to the camp. It was still night when we arrived. There were guards at the entrance gate who counted us once again.

The barbed-wire fence bore the picture of a skeleton skull with the warning: "Electrically charged." There was no escape. Stable-like barracks were lined up one after the other, each equipped with a huge searchlight that blinded our eyes. The stench of putrefaction entered our nostrils. Our feet sank into the mud, and we had to extricate ourselves anew with every step. There was no firm ground anywhere.

So this was to be our new home! A little farther back the sky was blood red. Giant flames were rising high in the air. At first it looked like fireworks. We gazed and gazed, not trusting our own eyes; there were people everywhere — people lying and people standing. The air was filled with anguished cries for help, with a heart-rending whimpering and wailing, with sounds that seemed animal rather than human. People had been dumped from the trucks like so much coal or dirt. They were beaten mercilessly; then the command was issued: "Hurry up! Get undressed! Hurry up! Faster! You're going to bathe." There they were standing naked in the winter's cold in high snow, their clothes rolled up in bundles, waiting for death. This picture defies description; not in my worst nightmares have I ever seen anything like it.

In an empty wooden barrack we sat down upon a pole and fell asleep. It was five o'clock in the morning when we were called. "Get up, you *Mistbiehnen* (manure bees) — but fast! You ought to be glad to be here. Your brothers have gone up the chimney already. Your turn will come, too." None of us showed what she felt at these words; all displayed perfect control, but our eyes were moist.

We lined up in alphabetical order. Then our numbers were tattooed on our left arms, with the remark, "Now you are only dirty numbers, nothing more. Your names will exist only in your memory." We were told we had no complaints coming, for now we were in the concentration camp and had to render strict obedience. If we did, nothing would happen to us; otherwise we would also go up in smoke, and only a black cloud would remain of us. These words were told us the first thing in the morning as a breakfast treat. We were all as white as sheets, for we knew we were lost if help did not come soon. It was especially emphasized that this was one of the largest annihilation camps in Germany. It was called Auschwitz-Birkenau, and five crematories were burning there day and night. The only time they were extinguished was when enemy airplanes were flying over Auschwitz.

We were given coffee, but every sip sank like a stone down our throats. They were soon shouting again: "All money and jewelry is to be surrendered!" Oh, how sad I was when I had to pull my engagement ring off my finger — the ring that had made me so proud and happy. I felt all empty inside, and I knew that all my dreams of love and happiness in the future were lost. I tried to hide a picture of my parents and my brothers and sisters, but they searched my pockets, and the photographs — the last ones I had — were torn up in front of my eyes. No document, no identification card could prove who I was, everything, without exception, went into the wastepaper basket. We all were praying to God for help.

Still we were not left alone. Once again we had to line up, five in a row. This time we were robbed of the last vestiges of our feminine pride: they cut off our hair and even shaved our heads bald. I did not recognize my own sister, so different was her appearance without hair. Although we were together, we did not know each other until we got used to the sight. Then the command was given to take off all clothes and lay them away. Nothing at all belonged to us any more. Then we were taken into the hallway of the shower rooms, which was terribly overheated. It was like a steam bath, about ninety-five degrees, while outside the temperature was below zero. In this *sauna* we had to remain for about an hour. We could hardly breathe in the heat. SS men were constantly walking through with their dogs and scrutinized the women who were at their mercy. After we were thoroughly heated through, we were then driven into the cold shower rooms, with their cold stone floors, where doors and windows were wide open on all sides, and the water was ice cold. Two SS men with dogs kept guard. Whoever tried to avoid the water was chased into the shower by one of the dogs, with a remark from the guard: "Let's hope you'll kick the bucket soon."

With blows, we were then driven from the shower rooms into the next room. There were no towels to dry ourselves with. We were trembling with cold. Finally, each of us received a man's undershirt, underpants, and a convict suit, no matter whether they were the right size or not. Heavy wooden shoes were thrown at our feet. But not only were we made to dress like criminals; the clothes we were given were also swarming with lice. All of us started to scratch ourselves immediately, and at first we thought it was just nervousness caused by all the irritations that were confronting us. Then I felt something moving up and down my body. My face flushed; I was ashamed of myself. I shook myself, and my skin grew ice cold. At that moment I really began to believe that man descended from the apes. Only then did I understand what it means to live like a human being and to be treated like one.

When we had finished dressing, we were told to line up, and again we were counted. A red triangle with a yellow line through it was given us to sew on our sleeves. Furthermore, the numbers that had been tattooed on our arms also had to be sewn on our sleeves. Each nationality had to display its own particular identification mark as a sleeve insignia, for among us were people from all the countries Hitler had invaded.

After we had received our numbers, we were marched back to our block. It was quite a job to march in those clumsy wooden shoes on the muddy ground. And what a sight confronted us on the way! Corpses were strewn all over the road; bodies were hanging from the barbed-wire fence; the sound of shots rang in the air continuously. Blazing flames shot into the sky; a giant smoke cloud ascended above them. Starving, emaciated human skeletons stumbled toward us, uttering incoherent sounds. They fell down right in front of our eyes, and lay there gasping out their last breath.

Here and there a hand tried to reach up, but when this happened an SS man came right away and stepped on it. Those who were merely exhausted were simply thrown on the dead pile. There they lay, about one to two hundred people on every block. Every night a truck came by, and all of them, dead or not, were thrown on it and taken to the crematory.

Once we came across a plump woman lying in the road. She had arrived in the camp only five days earlier. Her face and hands were completely covered with mud, with only the eyes showing. She called to us, "Help me! Oh, please help me! I am an opera singer from Berlin. You just can't let me die like this!" She told us her name, which I have since forgotten. Another dark voice sounded, the voice of a German SS woman: "Let the sow he." Most of us went past unaffected, as if none of this were of any concern; everyone feared for her own life only. Four women carried the former opera singer into one of the barracks, where she passed away during the night.

On our block — that is, in our stable-like barrack, which was to be our living quarters from then on — there was normally room for four hundred and fifty women. But now nine hundred women were crammed into those blocks. Triple-decker bunks, which were only plain wooden slats, served as beds. Ten to twelve of us shared one wooden board, with hardly enough room to sit, much less to lie. We found it necessary to put our dirty shoes, which were full of mud and dirt, under our heads at night, for otherwise they would have been stolen. Several of us had to share one blanket. We had to sleep in our day clothes, for it was cold, and we had nothing to change into. So through days and nights we did not get out of our clothes.

In rain, hail, or snow, we had to stand at attention during *Appell* (roll call). At 4 A.M. the alarm to get up was sounded. Sometimes it was raining so hard that we were drenched while standing at attention. Not having any change of clothes, we sometimes had to go to sleep in our wet things at night, and trembling with cold, we often could not find any sleep. Moreover, the lice and the fleas were pestering us terribly; they seemed as numberless as grains of sand on the beach. We could hardly fight them off; our clothes could have walked away by themselves.

I found it hard to believe that we were still in Europe, and sometimes I felt I had been carried away to some primitive island where I was forced to live like a savage. Many times I felt I must be dreaming, and I would call to myself: "Wake up! Wake up! You are having a nightmare!" I would look around me, trying to wake up, but alas, my eyes kept on seeing the same dismal picture. Finally, I would start to shake all over, and I would say to myself: "You are in a concentration camp, in an annihilation camp. Don't let them get you down." I didn't want to end up in the furnace; I wanted to live to tell of this, to tell how hundreds and thousands of my dear friends had met their end, and of what German culture had come to. And the Germans always believed that they were living on the very highest cultural level. As a child I often secretly, without permission, used to read murder mysteries and adventure stories about the Indians of the Wild West, but they were tame in comparison. Never had I read about anything so horrible as what I was seeing with my own eyes and living through myself.

When the whistle to *get* up sounded at 4 A.M., it was still dark, and we froze miserably. Water was scarce, and we could not even wash our faces a little. For breakfast we received a small cup of tea, so my sister and I, having two cups between us, drank one jointly and used the other to wash ourselves. We women had to carry heavy iron barrels that weighed up to one hundred and fifty pounds from the kitchen to the block. Before the carriers could reach their destination, they were attacked by the starving and thirsty people, and often a large part of the soup was accidentally dumped on the street in the shuffle, and seeped into the ground. The girls thought nothing of scooping up the food from the ground, together with the sand and dirt, fill their cups with this mixture, and take it to the block to eat there. On account of these attacks by the hungry ones, we usually received only about half of the amount of soup we were supposed to get, that is, half a quart instead of one quart for the main meal.

The hunger and the beatings increased day by day. Women and girls, in utter despair, ran in groups to the electrically charged wires, where they were caught like flies in a fly trap, and hung there. A few jerks, a shivering, a last nodding of the head, and their suffering was at an end. Wherever the eye reached one saw the dying and the dead. But still there were plenty of camp inmates, too many, in the opinion of the Germans. They took care that the number diminished even more rapidly.

The whistle to fall in for roll call had sounded again. Everyone stood at attention, almost without breathing, for the punishment for not complying with this order was to stand at attention without the slightest movement, without food, all day, or to kneel outside in zero or below-zero weather. Earlier, two German policewomen had thrown two girls into the lavatory pit and let them drown there. "Good riddance!" they had shouted hatefully.

During roll call that day the command was given for pregnant women to step forward; they would be given lighter work assignments, it was said. Their numbers were taken down. Two hours later, we saw them being taken to the crematory, where only a black cloud told of their fate.

We others were divided into different detachments. We were assigned to demolish shell-shattered houses, to dig ditches, to drive heavy lorries, to remove tree stumps, and to work on swampy grounds. We marched to and from our place of work accompanied by music. SS men and their dogs kept guard. There was no time for rest during working hours. When we returned to the camp at night, our bodies looked like the inside of a paint box. My head hurt so much from all the blows I had received that I was afraid of losing my mind. I had several dog bites on my hand.

One day, one of the girls, a companion from back home, fainted. An SS man, seeing her lying on the ground, came over and said, "Poor girl, are you tired? All right, you may lie there, and I'll cover you up." Then he picked up some rocks and threw them at the girl — at her face and body, wherever he could hit her. That afternoon, when it was time for us to go back to camp, he took away the stones, which were still covering her, and said, "I'll see if you are feeling better." She was still breathing. He lifted his heavy boot and stood with his whole weight on her chest, stamping down on her a few times, so that we could hear her ribs crack. Then he said, "Now you won't feel sick any more. You'll even be carried back to the camp." Some other girls had suffered a similar fate; they had already been collected.

Four of us then had to carry one of the bodies. The sister of one of the dead girls had to help carry her dear one, whose hair and forehead were still red with blood. Thus we marched: first the detachment, followed by us carrying eight or ten of our dead comrades. Arriving at the gate, with the music playing catchy march tunes, the SS women and men tried to suppress their laughter when we marched past them. It gave them satisfaction to watch us pass by, carrying the dead with their outstretched arms, our faces dirt-smudged by tears, some of us only half-dressed, our rags hanging down in tatters. Some of the girls no longer possessed shoes, their feet were dark blue and swollen. With deep wounds in their calves, and pus running down their legs, some were barely able to drag themselves on. Still there was shouting: "You dirty pigs! Walk faster or we'll teach you!" We did not know why we had to suffer so; our only answer was because we were Jews.

The wife of our chief rabbi from Breslau, Mrs. Lewin, who had always been a source of hope and courage, asked God for deliverance. She also had felt the heavy cudgels on her body, and she knew that only death could bring her the longed-for rest. A few days later, she was taken away. Her daughter Hanna died of spotted typhus (*Fleckfieber*) some time later.

It was already March, and the sun began to burn. There was no fat to protect our skin against sunburn. It became parched and wrinkled. Blisters formed on our faces. Only very slowly were we able to open our mouths, so painful was it to stretch the skin on our face. Our lips were covered with a black crust, and blood seeped out of the cracks. The soup that made up our dinner was so salty because of the bromine and soda in it that it was sometimes impossible for us to swallow it, for the mucous membrane in our mouths was painfully infected. From day to day we could see our comrades grow thinner and thinner. Many of them lost their minds and no longer could talk coherently. They would start to throw rocks and other objects at the SS men and even at their own friends. Bullets released them from their suffering. Our only words of hope were: "Girls, in three weeks everything will be over. Then we are going to start a new life." Desperately we clung to these words of consolation. But alas, we were destined to see one after another of our comrades carried away — shot, beaten to death, or mauled by the police dogs. It seemed that God had taken His hand from us.

The countless lice that plagued us so mercilessly, and the desperate scratching we resorted to, to find relief, caused carbuncles and other sores to develop on our bodies. Since we did not have enough water to wash ourselves, and never received a change of clothing, every second one of us contracted scabs. And constantly inspections were conducted in camp — that is, we were examined for all sorts of diseases, and if even an abscess was found, it meant death by gas chamber immediately.

Sundays were nonexistent for us. Even worse, a holiday was a sad day for us, for then new ways to torture us were tried out. On Sundays we had to carry large, heavy boulders from one place to another, until we were worn out with fatigue. Then the command was: "Line up! March! March!" While the commanding SS men watched in a group, we had to run as an endurance test for one whole hour. Whoever stumbled or got out of step was immediately taken out and separated from the group. If they did not like a face, or someone was still too fat, or too skinny, then she was taken out too. One day, my sister was among them. Out of five thousand women, about two thousand were called out during one endurance run. Later, these girls were taken to Block 25. This was the death block, whence the prisoners were taken to the gas chambers. My sister was able to get away just before line-up at Block 25, and managed to return to our block.

II

I FELT I could no longer stand these daily agitations, and, together with my sister, decided to run against the electric wires. Of the 198 Breslau women of our transport, there were only eighteen of us left, after three weeks. We were hoping that the end of the war would come soon, or else our own terrible end, rather than this state of never-ending terror.

Then one day, being a nurse, I was transferred to work in the so-called hospital buildings. There I had certain advantages. I no longer had to report for roll call. The beatings, too, were not quite as bad. The food was a little better. But in some ways it was worse. I soon adapted myself, but the work was very hard and most depressing. We had very few drugs and were short of bandages, so that even with the utmost economy the supply was not sufficient to go around. Although the medical men had obtained a plentiful supply of drugs from the various countries, they had been confiscated by the SS hospitals. It was not in the interest of the SS to supply prisoners with drugs to help them get well.

There was no sickness or contagious disease that did not attain epidemic proportions when it occurred in camp. There was no isolation ward, so that all the patients had to lie together, regardless of the nature of their illness. People, in fact, got worse in this so-called hospital instead of getting well. Spotted typhus, dysentery, scarlet fever, measles, diphtheria, scabby afflictions, surgical cases — all were thrown together. Surgical cases included those who had been mauled by dogs or wounded by cudgels, rifle butts, and rocks. Wounds of this kind were vast in number; one might have thought oneself in a human slaughterhouse. Most of the sick lay in their cots naked and dirty, with lice-infested blankets covering their wound-covered bodies. Purulent discharges and blood soaked the blankets, which had to be shared by eight to ten patients. They dirtied one another with their excrement, because they could not control their diarrhea. Fleas covered their bodies like so many caraway seeds. At night the floor was black with dead fleas. It is no exaggeration when I say that every evening I crushed hundreds of fleas from my own clothes alone. It reminded me of my childhood, when I used to watch the monkeys in the zoo delouse one another. Water was a precious commodity. About fifty people had to wash in one basin of water, and we nurses and doctors lacked sterilizing agents and soap in sufficient quantities to disinfect ourselves.

Upon me fell the task of accompanying one after another of my comrades to the gas-chamber block. When it was time to say good-by, I always told them we'd soon see one another again. Some of the girls asked me to relay their last greetings to their sisters, and to comfort them so that they would be strong in accepting their fate. At such times I suffered more than if I had received the most brutal beating, and whenever I could, I tried to hide somewhere to evade this job. Heavy blows on the head awaited me when I was found. Oh, how I suffered when a mother about to board the truck that was to take her to the gas chamber called to me: "I'm not afraid of death. No! On the contrary, at last I shall find peace. If only I could see my child once more, just press it to my heart once again, and know that someone would take care of it and raise it." This woman had been able, through the payment of a large sum of money and other valuables, to hide the child with farmers near Amsterdam. I tried to comfort her, saying that perhaps there was still a God after all, that orphans would be given a home again. But I myself was to learn that mother love can never, never be replaced.

At that time a mother and her daughter were both lying in the hospital block together. The mother died five days before the day set for their execution by gas chamber. The girl, who was fifteen years old, cried bitterly when she woke up one morning and found her mother dead beside her. Few of us were able to give the child a word of comfort, for with all the terrible happenings going on around us, most of us were concerned only for our own fate, by now. One of the nurses, who was a Slovak Jew, went over to the girl, saying, "Come on, get up and make your bed, or you'll die too," and she pulled the girl off the cot. Then four nurses came and pulled the dead mother out of her bunk while the girl watched. The woman's head hit the stone floor, and blood flowed from her mouth. Then the body was dragged over the floor and thrown together with the other corpses. The girl did not want to live any more, for now there was no one left who cared for her. Five days later she was picked for the gas chambers with the others. Whoever did not get well in the hospital within fourteen days, or at most three weeks, was doomed.

I had orders to use only the absolute minimum of paper bandages when dressing the wounds of the poor victims of the dogs' fangs and others who had been beaten into unconsciousness. The fingers of many of the girls were so chafed and sore from shoveling that the flesh hung loosely on the bones. Nevertheless I was told to be economical with the bandages. The girls had to continue shoveling with their barely usable hands until infection set in, or they volunteered for the gas chambers.

The hospital block was so crowded that no more patients could be admitted, and people had to be treated on an ambulatory basis. Large numbers of these unfortunates lay in front of the emergency station; some had sunk deep into the mud, others were gasping their last breath. Yet an SS man or a female guard passing by would take his cudgels and beat these already half-dead people shouting, "You lazy Jews! If you don't want to work, then we'll show you." Sometimes the poor wretches did not have enough strength left to scream or even to make a sound. Then the SS man would come to us in the ambulance and beat us up for permitting so many to register at the hospital, instead of sending them back to work. I often wished I could go back to outside work rather than stand by and watch so much suffering.

If a patient died during the night, then the rats, which abounded everywhere, would get at the body before it was cold, and eat the flesh in such a way that it was unrecognizable by morning. Sometimes only the bloody bones were left on the skeleton. The face was almost completely eaten away, which was a gruesome sight, enough to give anyone the shudders. So depressing was the work that I asked God to deliver me from it. As I watched a good friend and companion on her deathbed, I found myself actually envying her.

My sister came to me, crying, after standing at attention one day, and asked me to clean and bandage a dog bite she had received. The wound hurt me more than her. I had lost all desire to live. I said to her, "Let's go to the gas chambers together; we'll never get out of this hell alive."

But she implored me: "No, no. Have courage. We still want to live. We do believe in God, and perhaps He will send a miracle." She continued: "Today, we had to bring in eight or ten bodies of girls who didn't die from weakness during the day, but who were beaten to death by the troop leader and the female guards." All my sister's girl friends had died already, for this detachment, called "Buddi," was the very worst, and the most feared in Birkenau. My sister begged me to let her come to work in the hospital. I had been trying to get her transferred, but without success. I comforted her, and asked her to be patient for a few more days. But she only said: "I'm so very afraid of tomorrow." And crying, she left me.

The next day I fell ill and was running a fever of over 101 degrees. I was given permission to lie down. With a worried heart I waited for my sister, but she didn't come. A friend consoled me, saying that she had probably been transferred to a different troop, and that was the reason she couldn't come.

Days went by. I lay there with a high fever. Then one day the block eldest came. When I asked her where my sister was, she said, "Your sister is no longer with us; they brought her back dead from work one day." So she too had met her fate. Knowing that my mother had already been killed, and now my sister too, I begged God to let me die in my illness. But then the image of my brothers rose before me, and I thought: What would those boys ever do alone, spoiled as they had been by our mother? Perhaps they would survive; then what would they do alone? "You must live for them," a voice seemed to say to me. In my dreams I saw a vision of my mother with my brothers and sisters as they used to be, happy together, long ago. When I awoke I looked and looked until I realized that I was still in the concentration camp. I tried to suppress my longing, but the fever had taken hold of me.

More days passed. I was delirious. In my hallucinations I saw our commissar from Breslau, who said to me: "You came along of your own free will. You may go back home. I'll get your papers ready; then you may get up." I fell out of bed. They carried me back to my cot. Still delirious, I was waiting for my discharge from the camp, and so said good-by to my comrades in the bunks around me. But they told me: "Judith, you've gone mad. Pull yourself together. You're imagining things." I became very angry at these words, and if I hadn't been so weak I would have started a fight with them, for I felt that they were envious of my good fortune.

For three weeks I lay there hallucinating but not sleeping or dreaming. Then one day the fever went down, and I realized that I was still in the concentration camp and that liberation was impossible until the end of the war. Through rumors, we learned that because of the way matters stood at the front, things were beginning to look brighter for us. I was beginning to worry about how I would get home, for I was unable to walk a step. My legs were paralyzed. At times my hearing failed, and only by lip reading could I understand what was being said to me. My teeth were blackened by fever and thickly encrusted. I knew I had had spotted typhus. My thirst was almost unbearable, and I swapped my bread, which I could not eat anyway, for a glass of water. Even water had to be bought. Every week I felt a little better, but my legs still felt paralyzed. I was not even able to stand up beside my bunk for a few minutes. Even when holding on to something, everything would suddenly turn black before my eyes and I'd fall down.

Nurses and doctors were not included when selections for the gas chambers were made, thanks to Dr. Eva Boehm of Breslau, who spoke up for us courageously, and so saved our lives. Yet I could no longer believe I would ever get well again unless a miracle occurred. A miracle did happen, although it was six months before I could walk again. I knew no boredom during this time, for I dwelt on my memories of the past — of a life that seemed in retrospect like paradise.

It was already fall when I started to work again. One day a girl brought me news and greetings from my fiancé. Once again I felt that liberation must be near. All my thoughts were concentrated on being happy again, and forgetting the horror, or at least getting it over with somehow. I dreamed of happiness, and my desire to live became stronger and stronger.

Whenever I had an opportunity to talk to a male prisoner, I inquired about the whereabouts of my brothers. One day, I learned that two of them were working in the Buna factory. I was very happy to get this news, although I did not hear from them personally. But to my great sorrow I also learned, through some girls who were working in the office, that my youngest brother, Artur, had been gassed immediately upon arrival, together with my mother.

Since I was not required to stand at attention and was able to still my worst hunger pangs — for nurses and doctors were given extra rations, consisting of bread and a piece of sausage, twice a week — I became stronger with every day that passed, after my illness. But my work was terribly depressing. In two days I had to bandage 575-590 patients, for I had now been assigned as Verbandschwester (nurse for dressing wounds). Oh, the terrible and sad things my eyes were forced to see! One day, after the detachment had returned from work, a Jewish girl from Greece was brought to the hospital block. We hardly knew how to remove her clothes without hurting her too much, for the garments were virtually glued to her many wounds by dried blood. Only after her clothes were off did we see the extent of her injuries. She was quite confused and could not reply to our questions very well. But we learned that two police dogs had been set on her because she did not work fast enough. Her left buttock had been eaten off so that only tatters of flesh remained and the hipbone was visible.

Her pain was indescribable, and she wished only to die. Eight days later this girl was selected for the gas chamber.

Another girl, also Greek, suffered a similar fate. She, too, was brought to us in a frightful condition. The horrible experience had caused her to lose her speech. She could communicate with us only by sign languages or in writing. She had been taken into a private room by the *Rottenfuhrer* (troop leader), where he first beat her with his hands, then choked her until she got blue in the face. Then he had knocked out a few teeth, and finally took a sharp object and struck her with it, causing a deep gash in her head. The girl died the next day.

One day, an elderly woman came to the emergency ward. She begged us to admit her to the hospital for a few days, saying that she could not stand the beatings outside any longer. The poor old woman was blue and green all over. Because of the overcrowded conditions in the hospitals, we could accept only the most urgent cases, and the physician in charge denied her admission. The desperate woman prostrated herself before the doctor, and cried pitifully. I went over to help her up; she was obviously much older than the other prisoners.

Suddenly I recognized her, and I cried, "Chief Nurse Rosa! It is you!"

Then she remembered me, too. Her head trembling nervously, and with tears streaming down her face, she said, "I can't stand it any longer, yet five more days will I have to wait for death. I have already volunteered for the gas chamber, but it is overcrowded at the moment. Nobody can be accepted, voluntarily or not. They told me to come back in five days." She went on to tell me that the only reason she got into the camp was because she had been wearing her nurse's uniform when she was taken away. This woman had once been head nurse of the Breslau Home for the Aged, and her whole life had been one of duty and service for her fellow human beings. Now she was fifty-three years old, and concentration camp and gas chamber were her reward.

It happened frequently that Greek, Polish, and also German-Jewish girls were selected for the experimental hospital in Auschwitz. These girls were well taken care of there, and if they came through everything all right, and the German professor did not need them for a time, they would often return to us in the hospital block in Birkenau. Various operations were performed on these girls, such as the removal of the uterus and ovaries. On others, experiments in treating cancer by X rays were conducted, or there might be experiments in artificial insemination. Since new drugs were often tried out in the experiments, some of the girls were killed by the injections. At times the SS camp physician visited our block personally, and picked out the better-looking ones among the girls. Some knew right away what the purpose of this visit was, and there were always heartrending scenes when they were taken away to Auschwitz. Some girls' lives were saved in this manner, for they then were safe from death by gas chamber.

One day an SS man named Tauber visited our block in order to make selections for the gas chamber. He couldn't have been more than twenty-five years old. Thousands of women had to submit to being inspected by him, naked. When he entered our block we all had to stand at attention. The block eldest reported: "Block twenty-seven. Occupied by nine hundred and eighty prisoners!"

"Well, then, let's start right away," Tauber said. He pushed up his sleeves like a butcher getting ready to begin slaughtering. One after another, the patients had to march past him, and whoever was unable to stand was deposited naked on the stone floor. Again and again he kicked the patients with his nail-studded boots, in the belly or the back indifferently, until the blood ran. Of about nine hundred and fifty women, eight hundred were written down for the gas chamber. The block was almost emptied. The women prayed to God; they screamed for help; they prostrated themselves before the SS men, begging for their lives. Beatings were their answer.

The next day the trucks drove up, and we had to bring these unfortunates out naked. Some of them gave us their bread ration from the day before, which they had saved, asking us to keep it for them, for in their last hope they still believed a miracle might happen. One girl said tearfully, "Until now I still always had hope to see my brother in Palestine again. I cannot believe that this is to be my last hour and only ashes will remain of me." I tried to comfort her, but what could I say? Were there any words of comfort? I felt only that God had abandoned us. I sneaked away into a corner and dried my eyes, or I would have received a beating by the SS men who stood by the trucks, counting the girls to make sure none escaped. Some, being too weak, were unable to walk; others, who refused to enter the truck voluntarily, were pulled along naked by their hands and feet. The SS men shouted: "Heave ho!" and the male prisoners, with their help, would throw the emaciated patients onto the truck. One could hear the bones strike the boards as if they were pieces of wood. Some of the trucks made several trips back and forth. A few of the poor victims managed to wave good-by to us. Others were screaming, "Help us! Oh, please save us!" I was beginning to think that I myself was no longer among the living but was in the bowels of hell instead. When the trucks started to move away, frantic screams ascended toward the sky, and cries of "Father!" and "Mother!" were the last words we heard. Their hands extended heavenward, they were driven toward the crematory.

The rest of us were confined to our block. This meant that we were not allowed on the camp road. None of us talked, but our eyes were moist, for we felt that our turn to go to the gas chamber would come eventually. We looked out the small windows at the crematory. Soon we saw a huge, billowing cloud ascending. A giant flame leaped toward the sky, which remained blood-red for hours. I knew that my dear mother, my two sisters, and my brother Artur had met their deaths in this furnace. With a heavy sigh, I wondered what had become of my two older brothers. Were they still alive, or had the fire fed on them, too? "No," said a voice in my heart, "if this were so, then I wouldn't be able to stand any more. Then I belong with my mother and sisters." Thus I continued to live in the hope that some day I would be reunited with my brothers, so that we could bear our sad fate together and help one another forget.

One day, soon after the cremation of the patients, a large-scale selection took place at the camp. Five thousand women were picked out within three days to die in the gas chambers. These doomed ones were first transferred to Block 25. From there the prisoners were again assembled, then taken to the crematory. Completely naked, these unfortunates were forced to run along the camp road until they reached Block 25. Our male prisoners, who were at work shoveling sand, turned their eyes away sadly so as not to embarrass the women as they sped past them. But we women and girls no longer knew feelings of shame; long ago our sensibilities had been dulled to all things, decent or indecent. We knew that we did not have to be ashamed, but that the members of the SS should be, for their deeds of infamy.

These poor, death-bound victims were imprisoned on Block 25, which was enclosed by a stone fence on one side of the entrance. The small windows were barred, so that escape was impossible. Soup and coffee or tea were no longer given to them.

The poor people longed for water desperately. Thirst plagued them more than hunger, for they still had to wait from three to five days before death would release them. When it was raining, they would stretch their hand through the window bars, trying to catch a few raindrops to quench their thirst. Once, one of the girls who was still in her regular block and had so far escaped the gas chamber saw her sister holding out a cup in which to catch the rainwater. The girl went to the window and took the cup out of her sister's hand, in order to fill it for her. A female guard saw what was happening just as the girl was giving her sister the water and some bread. She shot down the girl on the spot, wounding her, then had her carried to the death block also.

One night, three days later, just as it was getting dark, we were again confined to our block. SS women and men came with long cudgels and clubbed the prisoners onto the trucks. They then accompanied them to the gas chambers, so that they could enjoy watching their misery to the full. Every time things went badly at the battle front — that is, when the army had suffered some kind of defeat — we knew it would be reflected in large-scale cremations at our camp.

One week later, there was another block barricade, and when we looked out our tiny window we saw fifteen trucks full of naked men from Auschwitz being driven to the gas chambers. Not in vain was our camp named Annihilation Camp Birkenau. (In this annihilation camp I was to spend two and a half years of my life, constantly fighting for survival). The men seemed in general to be calmer and more at peace with themselves, when being driven away, than the women. They sang the "Hatikvah" with their last ounce of strength. On another truck several were chanting: "*Schma, Jisroel, adonoj Elohenu, adonoj Achod.*" This means: "Eternal and incomparable is our Lord." Fifteen minutes later the crematory fires had ended their lives.

My heart beat rapidly all that day. Every bite of bread seemed to choke me. For the ghastly thought that one of my brothers might have been on one of those trucks would not leave me; or perhaps my fiancé, with whom I still hoped to find happiness some day, and together with him forget our sorrow in a better future. Perhaps the last wish of my brothers had been to see their sister once more. Yes, terrible thoughts crossed my mind. Every night I prayed to the dear Lord to protect at least my two brothers, since I already knew that my parents and my sisters were no longer alive, and only my brothers would be able to carry on and perpetuate our family. The thought of my brothers gave me the strength and will power to keep on living, and defiantly I said to myself: "The fire will not and shall not consume me! I'll remain with the last survivors. Nothing lasts forever. This rule of infamy will also come to an end, some day."

I thought of how, when the people in the ancient land of Shimar wanted to build the Tower of Babel, which was to reach up to the sky, the Lord caused it to collapse because it was getting too tall. So I said to myself: "Be strong. These horrors, too, will not grow into the sky. The Lord will one day destroy them." Although in our hearts we no longer believed in liberation, we encouraged each other by quoting passages from the Bible. History reveals that pogroms of the Jews have taken place time and again through the centuries, but I don't believe that such intense and large-scale persecutions have ever before occurred, and certainly not in recent centuries, and on a civilized continent. This era shall be one of eternal shame for Germany.

One night we could not sleep; we heard constant shooting outside. There was loud screaming, running and driving back and forth. New transports had arrived from Poland. The people knew that they were on their way to the gas chambers, for they saw the crematory burning on three sides, and they were all familiar with these furnaces from other German camps in Poland. They attacked the SS men with knives. Some of them even had revolvers, and used them, and six SS men were killed. But soon the SS received help, and twenty truckfuls of Jews were shot with machine guns that night. On top of every truckful of corpses they put one live Jew, and this load was dumped right in front of our shoe room, which was near the crematory, so that the bodies lay there in a house-high pile, in full view. There they remained for three days, since other shipments were being received from Poland, and the living had to be gassed first. Out of about one thousand people, only a hundred or so were accepted into the camp.

The crematory, which was operated at maximum capacity, burned at three different places. A dentist was employed to pull the gold teeth of the gas-chamber victims, who usually were only unconscious. Ten at a time, they were laid on a dolly and thrown into the fire. Jewish prisoners were working in the crematories. Their job was to burn the gas-chamber victims. About three hundred of them worked in the five crematories. It often happened that a prisoner employed there found himself confronted with the task of putting into the fire his own mother or sister, who may have arrived on a later transport. Sometimes the workers threw themselves in alive. This special detachment received first-class food, which even included chocolate and wine. These delicious treats were what the poor dead victims had brought with them from home. The prisoners liked to drink themselves into oblivion in order to forget the human slaughter. But they did not hold their jobs for more than three months. At the end of this period they were relieved, to make sure they could not tell too much. They were told that they were going to join a working detachment. But unfortunately they were destined to join the detachment to heaven instead. In a bathroom, where they were told to change their clothes, they were quietly gassed, then burned. Yes, the poor Germans must have had a very high gas bill in those days.

The fat of the dead bodies was utilized in the manufacture of soap. The war soap that was generally sold bore the letters RIF, which stands for *Ruhe in Frieden* (Rest in Peace). The rest of the ashes was thrown into the river. If someone had interesting tattooing on his body, a lampshade would be made out of his skin, and it would then grace the room of the block leader. If a victim had beautiful teeth, someone would keep the skull in order to display it on his desk. Shudderingly I thought of one of my brothers whose teeth had been knocked out in a boxing match, when he was still at home. All his front teeth were of gold, and whoever had gold teeth in his mouth was doomed right away, just for the sake of the gold, which they needed badly. Thus my thoughts were always dark and gloomy about this brother.

Again a major inspection took place on our block. The SS camp physician, Dr. Rothe, came personally. The SS watched closely to make sure nobody hid under the straw or managed to put on nurse's clothes as a disguise. Since at that time I still looked quite ill after my bout with typhus, the camp physician asked me, "Who are you?" I replied that I was the nurse in charge of dressings in the block. Then he asked where I came from, and I told him from Breslau. His next question was, "Why are you here?"

"Because I am a Jew," I answered. Then I took courage and asked him to give me some lighter work, so that I could regain my strength faster. He asked if I had had any experience with children, and I replied that I had taken care of children and infants for a long time, when I was in the hospital back home. Then he announced that starting the following week I would work on the Russian children's block. I thanked him, for I knew that I would be better off there; the work would be easier and the food a little better.

But first I had to help to take those selected to the death block. They were, for the most part, only skeletons. I longed to be on the other block, so I would no longer have to witness so much suffering. I had been ordered to carry on my back, to Block 25, one of my best friends, who was from Berlin. Clad in a blanket, she weighed no more than sixty pounds. I had at first refused to carry this friend, who was so close to me, to that place. But she herself begged me to carry her because she did not want to be dragged naked, by her hands and feet, along the floor. On Block 25 she was laid on the cold stone floor with the others, where they had to wait until trucks were available to carry them to the crematory.

It was very cold, and it was raining. Some of the patients died before they even reached the gas chambers. Many of them were covered all over with excrement, for there were no sanitary facilities, and they could not keep themselves clean because of diarrhea. Some were holding on to their last piece of bread, which was worth more in camp than gold or diamonds in the outside world. Naked, their last piece of bread in their hands, they were driven toward the crematory. The survivors ate any remaining bread that was left behind, even if the sick had lain on it and it was covered with excrement. I confess that oftentimes I myself pulled a piece of bread from under a dead body, even though the corpse had lain on it all night. So great was our hunger that we were even capable of eating dirt. Whoever has not lived through a horror like this will never be able to understand what it means to go hungry, and how it hurts. I often nibbled at my own skin and my nails, because my stomach was growling so that I could not go to sleep. Many times I thought of how people elsewhere were living in freedom and could sit down to a table laden with good things and enjoy luscious meals. I would have been only too glad to have had just the spoiled and stale foods from such a table. Why is life so unfair? I thought. One man gorges himself while another starves. What terrible sins had we committed to be destined to die such a death? I knew that I had done no wrong and was suffering for my religion only. I remembered the old saying: "God's mill grinds slow, but sure." One day God would grow angry at this suffering, and the page would be turned. It is easy to wage war and raise weapons against the sick and the helpless who cannot defend themselves; in fact, it is the greatest cowardice one can imagine. The SS men knew perfectly well that it was safe to shoot on this battlefield, for there was no one who could resist. They should have tried to prove instead that they were able to win the war against an enemy stronger than we. But, oh, how they trembled when hundreds of airplanes circled overhead. The furnaces were put out immediately, and the SS, together with the commandants, took refuge in our camp, which they knew the bombers would not attack. No sooner were the air raids over, however, they were once again the mighty ones, who could not tell us often enough how we would all end up "where we belonged." Such words meant nothing to us at this stage, for we were no longer afraid of death, and would be able to bear the fate that had already been shared by thousands of our brothers.

III

ON THE children's block where I worked there were only Russian children. Every day some of them died because they had no resistance against the various diseases. By order of the SS, we were allowed to speak only German with the children. One child, who was suffering from hydrocephalus, said nothing but "Hail, Stalin." We had to keep this child constantly hidden, for had the SS heard this expression just once it would have meant instant death for the child.

One day a little Jewish boy from Holland arrived with the Russian children. We impressed upon the child that, if anyone asked him, he must say he was Russian. He understood us quite well, for he replied, "I know; otherwise they'll put me in the furnace." Every time the commanding officer entered the camp, he would ask, "Are there any Jewish children here?" And every time our reply would be negative. Thus we lived in constant fear for the child's life.

When I asked him about his mother, he said, "I don't know if Mommy is still alive, for if she were she would have come for me long ago; but Daddy must be, for he is very strong. Mommy could have left me in Holland. But she did not want me to be left behind alone." Everybody brought food for the child so that he would not go hungry.

Soon the boy became ill with typhus. He said to us, "Never mind if I have to die. It is beautiful in heaven, too. Mommy told me about it. The angels have beautiful flowers and gardens." Every day the child wasted away more and more. Even the German block eldest could not hide her tears. After a few days he was gone. We put his body on a stretcher that we had decorated with flowers and carried him to the death house ourselves.

I had been working in the children's block for six months when one day it was announced that the children were to be sent to a children's home in Lamberg. The Russian mothers threw themselves on the ground, screamed, and hugged their children desperately. But pitilessly the SS tore the little ones away from them. Within three days, five thousand Ukrainian children were loaded on a truck and driven to Crematory No. 4, which was located in a little wooded area. We watched the flames as they illuminated the sky above the woods.

Shortly before Christmas, another large-scale inspection took place in both the women's and the men's camp. Again five thousand female prisoners were picked out for the gas chambers. They selected the strongest of the men, because they feared a rebellion might take place soon, a rumor that a Polish prisoner had spread. The men had decided to try a revolt because of the constant and never-ending cremations. It was exactly one day before Holy Eve. The Christmas tree, decked with many electric lights, was alight on the camp road. The Christian girls were singing Christmas carols. Suddenly the word was: "Block barricade." A little later we saw twelve truckfuls of naked Jewish men being driven to the crematory. It was very cold, and the snow glistened in the light. With strong voices, the men sang; their last song was the "Hatikvah." We, the last ones surviving, had little hope left that we would live to tell the world how thousands of our brothers had met with death.

I had almost despaired when on my last birthday I learned that my fiancé had died of typhus. So this was the final chapter of a man who, in his whole life, had only known kindness to his fellow man, and work and duty. I had only my two brothers left now. My parents, my sisters, and my fiancé were beyond suffering. All my hopes of still finding happiness once more, after all this, were now over. My heart felt as though it were full of heavy rocks that seemed to be getting heavier and heavier.

Two days after Christmas, a Jewish child was born on our block. How happy I was when I saw this tiny baby. It was a boy, and the mother had been told that he would be taken care of. Three hours later, I saw a small package wrapped in cheese cloth lying on a wooden bench. Suddenly it moved. A Jewish girl employed as a clerk came over, carrying a pan of cold water. She whispered to me, "Hush! Quiet! Go away!" But I remained, for I could not understand what she had in mind. She picked up the little package — it was the baby, of course — and it started to cry with a thin little voice. She took the infant and submerged its little body in the cold water. My heart beat wildly in agitation. I wanted to shout "Murderess!" but I had to keep quiet and could not tell anyone. The baby swallowed and gurgled, its little voice chittering like a small bird, until its breath became shorter and shorter. The woman held its head in the water. After about eight minutes the breathing stopped. The woman picked it up, wrapped it up again, and put it with the other corpses. Then she said to me, "We had to save the mother; otherwise she would have gone to the gas chamber." This girl had learned well from the SS and had become a murderess herself. There were also many Jewish block eldests who sold the lives of their own people to protect their personal safety.

It was in January, 1944, when another inspection of the typhus patients took place. Marianne Lattner, my last surviving colleague from our Breslau Jewish hospital, was one of the sick. She had nearly recovered but was still weak; in another two days or so she would be all right. That afternoon I visited her, taking her something to eat. As soon as she caught sight of me, she called out, "Judith, I've been selected for the gas chamber; but I won't go there while I'm alive. You *must* get me some pills so I can drug myself." She began to sob uncontrollably.

I rushed to the office of the troop leader, who listened to my story. I told him that this girl was my only cousin and implored him to save her life. He asked for her number, saying that he would cross it off the list when it was returned by the political division. Happily I returned to my friend to give her the good news. "Marianne, you are safe!"

She put her arms around me and vowed, "We shall remain together as long as we live."

The date for the transport to the gas chambers had been set for Saturday. However, since quite a few protests had been received, Camp Commander Kramer ordered it to be dispatched two days sooner. When my friend heard about this, she screamed for help and cried out in despair. Immediately she sent another girl to tell me what had happened.

I ran back to the troop leader right away, to beg for the girl's life once more, but in my excitement I didn't notice that it was not the same one. "Sir," I blurted out breathlessly, "my cousin has been included in the transport after all!"

He looked at me and said, "Now, then, let's have your number. If things displease you around here you'd better go along too."

I had to read off the number on my arm, which a clerk took down. My heart seemed to have stopped beating, and I could only think that I probably wouldn't have to suffer very long when inhaling the gas. I told myself how soon everything would be behind me and all misery would have an end. Suddenly the clerk looked up at me, and said, "Are you crazy? Get out of here at once!" I ran as fast as I could. She followed, hugged me gently, and said, "You can still go on living. Soon the war will be over and we'll be liberated. You are still so young, and none of us has any relatives any more." She went on to tell me that she had torn up my number. I took a deep breath, and thanked her with tears in my eyes.

So my last friend from Breslau had also been consumed by the flames. Her block eldest gave me her last greeting, and told me that she had hoped to be saved until the very last moment. For weeks I could not find peace within myself, because I kept thinking that Marianne must have thought that I had done nothing for her, and had been only trying to quiet her with promises of safety.

There was no end to the worrying and excitement. When I was a small child, my mother told me about heaven and hell, but I believe now that it must have been a form of hell on earth that we lived through, and that all our sins have already been absolved here. Hell could not possibly be worse than this.

A few days later, word got around that all Jewish employees were to be discharged from the hospital. I knew that outside work meant certain death, for no one could stand it for more than eight weeks. Then one's strength would give, and anyone who was no longer productive would be sent to the gas chambers.

One day the whole camp had to stand at attention from early morning till late in the afternoon; that is, actually we had to kneel down with raised hands, and squat on the ground without moving. A number froze to death that day, and most of us were frozen stiff that night. A large number fainted during the ordeal. It was not possible to arouse any feelings of pity, for we were all Jews, or other prisoners hostile to Germany.

I was sure that if I were assigned to an outside detachment, I would never live to see my long-dreamed-of and hard-fought-for freedom again. Forty were retained; the rest of us were discharged from the hospital and taken into the *sauna* to change. Suddenly Lagerfuhrer (Camp Leader) Hessler appeared to select prisoners for work in the Union Factory, an ammunition plant. All of us were very glad to get into a good detachment, where there was at least some chance of survival. Of course, we knew that the extra food rations were not given out of love for us, but to improve the quality of our work, or, in other words, for the sake of the military. Jewish workers were preferred for jobs of this kind, because they seemed to be more dependable. Camp Leader Hessler picked only the healthiest and strongest girls for this work. He asked whether we had already had typhus, for in an ammunition plant they could not afford frequent replacements, because too much time would be lost. We had to present ourselves naked before Camp Leader Hessler, to have him inspect us. Anyone displaying scabs or other skin diseases was eliminated. My friend and companion Frieda Hochster was taken out because she had several boils caused by vitamin deficiency. Sadly we parted from each other. My heart was beating fearfully when I said good-by to my friend, for we did not know what would be the fate of those afflicted with skin diseases.

Full of anxiety and worry, these girls returned to Block 8. Shortly thereafter there was a selection, and my friend Frieda was picked for the gas chambers. There was no one who could help her. Her last hope was to go to the camp physician herself and to beg for her life. After she had waited for Dr. Klein all day, in bitter cold and without food, his reply was (she was prematurely gray because of the horrors of camp existence): "You are old enough to die. What the others can stand, you can take also." Since it was not his life that was at stake and only — as he looked at it — the life of a worthless Jewess was involved, his verdict was an easy one to arrive at.

Although Frieda, deep down inside, had already drawn the balance line under her life and had accepted everything passively, even objectively — as if it were just another sad Jewish fate rather than her own — she still felt a deep horror for the gas-chamber death. So she went once more to Camp Leader Hessler and begged him to save her life. But he replied: "I can't help you either. It makes no difference whether you die sooner or later."

Then she said: "It's only that I would love to keep on working a little longer. It makes no difference what I do; I've spent my whole life working." She continued to tell him how her husband had fought for Germany during World War I and had even been cited for distinguished service.

He looked at her, and asked, "Where do you come from?"

"From Osnabruck, sir."

"Give me your number. You'll be taken off the list. Return to your block." Those were his words. Overjoyed, half-laughing, half-crying, she ran back to her block. Yet later, when the death-bound women were loaded onto the trucks, her name was among them. They were already pulling her clothes off, to throw her on the truck with the others, when with her last remaining strength she screamed, *"Herr Lagerfuhrer! Herr Lagerfuhrer!"* She yelled so loudly that she damaged her vocal cords, and consequently lost her voice for a few days. The camp leader had recognized her, however, and asked, "Are you the one from Osnabruck? Be off!"

So she was actually saved after all her agitation. They led her back to the block, where she suffered from severe heart palpitations for several days.

This friend of mine is one of the few survivors who lived through the hard times of 1942 in Birkenau, a period that it was almost impossible to live through. Today, we can talk about this suffering, when death was uppermost in our minds every day, with shudders and yet with pride. And the starving and the beatings were just as bad as the fear of death every day. How often I wished just once more to be able to satisfy my hunger and then to die — just once more to have a bowlful of potatoes all for myself.

In the meantime, I was already working in the ammunition plant. The manager assigned me to a very exacting and important job. As I had been instructed by a lieutenant, I had to check the explosives for minute defects. These shells had already passed through fifteen previous inspections, and mine was the last and the most important one. This work made me very nervous and fearful, since I had to be in contact with the managing director, the captain, the officers, and the foreman. They never could agree on anything among themselves, and so I never knew to whom to listen. The foreman wanted to supply as much material as possible; the director wanted to send as much as possible to the front; and the captain did not want to okay anything that showed even the most microscopic flaw. But when complaints from Berlin were received, it was always the prisoner who was at fault. Several times every week I was told that I would be sent to the crematory for sabotage. I feared death less than the beatings.

Once when a complaint had been received a second time, our whole checking department of eighteen girls had to do exercises for a whole hour after returning to the camp. Up, down, up, down — we had to lie flat on the ground and get up again. Another time we each were to receive twenty-five lashes. One of the officers who still had some pity for us rejected this punishment, saying it was not in the interest of our work. Not a day passed when I didn't have cause to cry. Our only consolation was that we knew the day of our liberation was getting closer and closer.

Sometimes the foremen accidentally — or purposely left a newspaper lying around so that we were able to catch a glimpse of the reports from the battlefronts. The faces and moods of the directors and managers also gave us a clue to the way things stood. The air raids over Auschwitz grew heavier all the time, and we feared for the lives of the two thousand prisoners working there. Sometimes, when the alarms took place during the day, everything just stopped.

One day I became ill with a septic sore throat, or perhaps it was diphtheria, and I had to enter the hospital as a patient. Once again God saved me. Two days before a large-scale inspection took place, I was discharged and sent back to the working block.

During my absence from my job, another girl had been trained to take my place. But the woman physician on the night shift happened to be discharged just then because of a prison term she had to serve. So I had the good fortune to be assigned as nurse in the first-aid station of the plant. I was very glad that I no longer had anything to do with the foreman, the lieutenant, and the rest of the plant management.

We were very busy in this emergency ward, for we had to take care not only of all first-aid cases but also of all further treatments of wounds. Every night we handled between twenty and thirty accidents. An accident happens fast if the prisoner is overtired. Every night several of the workers lost two or three fingers. Even such accidents were regarded as sabotage, and it frequently happened that an accident victim received a beating from the commanding officer in addition to her injury. Quite a few of the machines were out of order, and the mechanics were unable to repair some of the parts. Yet the machines had to be kept running in order to produce the work that had to be delivered. As the troop leader used to say, it was better to lose a few Jews than to have production curtailed. Often the trains were delayed, and the prisoners were consequently not able to deliver ten thousand explosives per night.

As the setbacks at the battlefront grew more serious, the nasty moods of the SS increased too. The commanding officer took several of the prisoners into his private room, one by one, and beat them so violently that the walls and ceiling were spattered with blood; then he felt better, and sent the prisoners back to their jobs. The men came to us in the emergency ward to have their wounds dressed. They were afraid to tell us how they were hurt. A little later the troop leader would come and ask us what had happened to the prisoners. The physician and I said there had been an accident at the plant. Then he went over to them and checked, to see whether they were back at work.

The people were so emaciated that every blow they received hurt twice as much. If they had a piece of bread with a pat of margarine and a small onion, it was a most delectable supper for them, and I myself remember that it tasted as good to me as had roast goose in the good old times. We were very economical with the onion, making it last for two meals. Oh, it was just delicious, and if we also had a little salt to boot it was enough to make us completely satisfied.

One day a prisoner who had a dry scab in his beard came to us for treatment. Just then a very young commanding officer stepped in. He took one look at the prisoner, and said, "And this is still alive? You should have been turned into soap long ago!" He took down his number. Two days later the prisoner was missing when his detachment left for work. There was no question of what had become of him.

Every morning when we were getting ready to march back into camp at Birkenau, our hearts were filled with uncertainty and fear. "We lived through the night, but what will the day bring us?" we always asked ourselves. Huge flames flared up against the sky every morning. We saw trucks, one behind the other, being driven toward the crematory. The prisoners sometimes waved to us from afar. Little did they know where they were going! We would enter the camp, singing. The smell of rotted flesh was in the air. We sighed; would we ever breathe pure air again?

Across from us, on the other side of the camp, the new arrivals were getting undressed. Naked, their clothes rolled into bundles, they were led into the gas chambers. Blows were directed at any part of the body, if someone was not fast enough. "You will bathe now," the executioners told them. But never again did we see them. The fire sealed their destiny.

At four o'clock in the afternoon we were awakened to get ready for work on the night shift. The crematories were still burning. We started to move out. More truckfuls of new victims were arriving. They were transports from Greece and France, and they had no idea that they had been brought this far away from their homeland just to be killed. They had been told they would be put to work. Constantly transports from all the German-occupied countries arrived. It was June, 1944, and work had been accelerated to the utmost. The prisoners had to lay railroad tracks from the freight depot — which consisted of a large empty area and was not an official depot — all the way into the camp and directly to the crematory. This work of carrying stones and laying tracks was carried on at a rapid pace until darkness set in. Yes, we slaves had to build our own road to death. Thus the seemingly endless chain of freight trains went right up to the crematory, where each car was emptied, one after another, and its contents sent to certain death by gas and fire.

At about this time one hundred thousand Hungarian Jews were reported to be on the way, and they began to arrive daily. We almost despaired when we observed the length of these trains as they moved in, and saw children and grown-ups wave to us in the belief that, no matter how hard it had been in the past, they had nevertheless managed to save their lives, after all. We hung our heads and wiped away our tears.

One afternoon, when after roll call we once again were on the march to the night shift in the ammunition plant, another long train full of victims arrived. The locomotive had been uncoupled and was just departing through the gate. At that moment a car arrived with a committee of SS men who were going to decide on the spot who of these people was to live and who was to die. The automobile carrying the executioners approached the gate just as the locomotive was passing through, and there was a terrible collision, for the car ploughed into the locomotive head on. We heard the crash, and then saw the car lying underneath the locomotive. The sirens immediately sounded the alarm, and emergency squads rushed to the scene. Two hours later, the car was still pinned under the locomotive; they had not yet been able to pull it free. Two of the SS men were killed instantly, and three others who had sustained injuries had been taken to the hospital. We took a deep breath, and felt for the first time that there was justice in the world after all.

The transports kept coming in. The furnaces were burning day and night, without interruption, at maximum capacity. The sky was blood red. The whole camp smelled of smoldering bones. Even when eating we could not escape the stench, which reminded us that the food we were eating was probably what our dead brothers had brought with them as emergency rations, in the belief that they would have to take care of their own food supply during the first few days in camp.

The children ran about and played in the sand while their parents got undressed at the command of the executioners. They were to get ready "to bathe." Everyone was very thirsty after the long train ride. They were told: "Soon now you'll be taken into the kitchen. There you'll be given food and drink." Some asked fearfully about the nature of the flames they could see leaping out of the chimney tops. The reply was: "That's the factory where you'll be working from now on." We watched the children play. They formed a circle and danced — some very small ones, others a little bigger, children so lovely and sweet it almost tore one's heart out to think that their life span would be cut off in just a few minutes or hours. A mother would have been only too glad to give up her own life, could she have saved that of her child by it. Nobody would have thought it possible that in civilized Europe this was possible — the murder of innocent women and children.

Still the transports kept coming in, with short intervals in between, so that the crematories were no longer sufficient and could not absorb the increasing influx. But the murderers soon found a way out. They had several pits dug and filled with wood brought from the forest. Over this they poured gasoline. The ambulances supplied the gasoline. And the people were pushed into the pits to burn there. Many of the children were thrown in alive. Someone would grab a child's arms, another his legs, and thus little babies were hurled through the air like a length of wood, to land in the blazing pit, while the murderers watched the results of their bravery with great pleasure. They also enjoyed throwing children alive into a pond that adjoined one of the crematories.

All that remained of the victims were their shoes and clothes rolled up in bundles, which a special detachment of prisoners had to sort out. Quite a bit of food was still found there, too, which the prisoners assigned to this job quickly ate. I was reminded of the quotation: "One man's death is another's bread." In this way a few of the starving ones could at least fill their bellies for once.

Those whose lives had been spared were put into prisoners' garb and their hair was shaved off. All their belongings had to be turned over, including rings and watches. Clad in wooden shoes, some of them barefooted, they were loaded like cattle into stock cars and sent to Germany and other countries. Very young Hitler Youth boys no more than fifteen years of age guarded these girls with rifles. These unmannerly and uncouth Hitler Youth boys felt elated at the chance to play the master to so many female prisoners.; Again we asked ourselves: "Will the day come when these slave dealers shall receive their just punishment? Will there ever be a change, or will our brothers and sisters in other countries never find out what happened to us?" Oh, how it hurt when I watched our men, misery and hunger written on their thin faces, when they went to the manure piles and searched in them for the moldy and spoiled bread crusts that the Polish and Ukrainian girls, who were able to receive gift parcels, had thrown away. They gulped down these moldy leftovers ravenously. Some of them wished they were pigs, for then they would have a warm pen and regular feedings of potatoes. We even would have been satisfied with the potato peelings. One day while I was watching the hogs in Auschwitz, I suddenly found myself thinking how nice it would be to be a pig and to be able to still my hunger cravings for once.

With all our troubles we still had to sing while marching. Morning, noon, and night, constantly my ears rang with the commands: "Left, right, left, right. Get up, you sluts! March! March!" I could not even imagine any more how it felt to walk on a sidewalk and to stop when I wanted to. Even when going to sleep we were told to lie on our sides so that six or eight of us would find room on one cot. This was not easily done, for we could hardly stretch out our legs. And constantly bedbugs promenaded up and down our bodies and over our faces. We were much too exhausted to find the strength to fight them any more. Nothing mattered anyway. A few more fleas, a few more lice, a few more bedbugs — what difference did it make? We had to keep our dirty wooden shoes under our heads, or we would have had to march out barefooted the next day.

Every day we passed a nursery where the most gorgeous roses and other flowers in all colors were blooming. The sun was shining brightly and warmed us pleasantly. I thought how beautiful the world was, but not for us. "Perhaps the sun is shining for us, too..." I once said to my girl friend, who was like a sister to me. The roses were beautiful and seemed to smile at us with their lovely colors. My thoughts wandered: perhaps they were bringing me greetings from my loved ones... they might even be fed by the ashes of my mother or sister. These lovely, exquisite roses seemed to be looking at us; it was as though they were trying to tell us something. Every time we marched out I was glad to pass by the nursery. I knew that the soil around Auschwitz had been saturated with blood, and perhaps it had also been fertilized with the ashes of our dead.

Everything in Auschwitz had been stolen from foreign nations, which the Germans had raided like common pirates. Auschwitz was a treasure house of gold and diamonds stolen from the living and the dead. The SS women displayed the most expensive and elegant jewelry. Often they carried out suitcases full of gold and diamonds and buried them. They were not allowed to take what they wanted, for everything belonged to the government and the very highest Nazi pigs — I cannot think of another name for them.

Once a very beautiful girl from Poland aroused the sympathy of an SS man. He obtained a guard's uniform for her and managed to sneak her out of the camp at night. At roll call the next morning it became evident that the girl was missing. Her first name was Mala; I've forgotten the other.

After we had been standing there for a long time and had been recounted, the sirens sounded the alarm, and with the help of the secret police they soon located the girl not far from Auschwitz.

They took her into the bunker at Auschwitz, where she was beaten and miserably tortured, to make her reveal who had helped her escape. They put clamps on her fingernails, repeatedly poured cold water over her, and hung her up with her head downward until she told who it was.

When we were entering the camp, after our night shift that day, we met Mala as she was being taken to Camp Birkenau, guarded by an SS man. We were not allowed to talk to her. She looked at us with a hunted look in her eyes, like a deer pursued, and her expression told us that she knew what was going to happen to her. As soon as we entered the camp we saw that the gallows had been erected in the middle of the camp road, and we knew that Mala was to die by hanging. Our hearts were beating loudly, and we shuddered at the thought that we might have to witness it.

Hardly two hours had passed when we were called to stand at attention. All detachments took their places, and several thousand girls stood there by the camp road as quiet as mice, hardly daring to breathe. Then they brought Mala and placed her on a chair in front of the gallows. The commanding officer made a speech, telling us that anyone of us who tried to escape would suffer the same fate. While he was talking, we saw that Mala, whose back was turned to us, had a razor blade with which she was trying to cut her veins. One of the officers noticed the blood and, running over to her, turned her arm around. Mala with her other arm dealt him a tremendous blow. Another SS man broke her arm on the spot. The girl was completely exhausted, due to the severe loss of blood. Now they first had to send her to the emergency ward to stop the heavy bleeding. She could no longer stand up, and a car had to be obtained to take her away.

After this incident her punishment was to be twice as severe, and they were also planning to throw her into the furnace alive. Prisoners under guard had to drive her to the crematory. But one of the officers there recognized her, for she had once worked in his detachment. He took pity on her and let her have a bullet first. We were glad to hear that she was not burned alive, when our comrades told us of her death.

The suffering, the fear, and the worry never stopped. Every morning when we marched in we saw new victims arriving. One time they were transports from Poland, where they were dissolving the ghettos. The people on the trucks were hollow-cheeked and bony, and they themselves had to collect the brush that fed the fires that burned them to death in the pits. The poor wretches knew that their time had come. Neither word nor smile was on their lips any longer. We were all hoping the Allied bombs would hit the camp, so that everything would be over for us.

For the second time it happened that SS guards in groups of eight and ten had escaped to Poland. They probably sensed that the war was nearing its end, and they were ashamed, because of the gruesome murdering of people that they had to witness daily.

We learned from the newly arriving transports that things were steadily getting worse for the Germans. I was already planning how to get back home, and the thought of being reunited with my brothers after such a long separation made me quite content. I kept thinking of all the nice things I would do for my brothers, and of starting a new life together. Since I had not heard anything from them for quite some time, I asked our prisoner-physician from the plant to try to find out for me how they were, and to give them my love, if possible. I gave him a few lines in writing, telling them our dear mother, our sister Herta, and I were all counting the days until we could be reunited. "With love… be brave and do what you can to survive; for Mommy must see you again…" I did not want them to know that my mother and my sister Herta had died long ago.

A few days later the prisoner-doctor was able to learn of my brothers' fate. He told me that my oldest brother, Sally, who had just turned twenty-six, had been taken to the gas chambers in Birkenau in January of that year. This was the worst thing that could have happened to me. I cried during working hours, and the foremen and the female guard asked me what was the matter. I told them that all of a sudden I had been gripped by an uncontrollable feeling of homesickness, for had I told them the real reason, that would have caused the doctor serious trouble. I could not face the fact that now there was only my brother Siegfried left alive. I quietly prayed to God to protect and keep this last one of my family, and to give him strength and solace to live through this hard time. I wished I could be near him and talk to him. "Be strong, soon all will be over; I love you dearly, my brother," I wanted to say. Oh, if I could only kiss him once more. I thought my heart was tearing apart. I prayed voicelessly: "Dear God, please let it end; let it be enough. It can't go on. Yes, an end, any kind of end; it doesn't matter which — whether ours or the Germans." I felt that I could stand no more. I cried for days and nights. My eyes were red and swollen.

That Sunday the prisoners gave a beautiful concert with violins, mandolins, and cellos. The violins seemed to cry with me, and again I felt that my heart was tearing apart. The sun was smiling down on us, but it no longer shone for me; my heart was dark and empty. I didn't want to eat, and friends and comrades tried in vain to cheer me up. I was barely able to drag myself about; my feet had become heavy, as though they could no longer carry me. It was a long time before I recovered from the blow I had received. It was all to the good that I had to march out to work every day and was kept busy all the time.

Several former opera singers from Greece were employed in the plant as machinists. When the female guards were in a good mood, they let them sing for them some of their songs in Greek or other languages. Their voices filled the whole plant when they sang "Mamma" or "La Paloma." For this they received an apple or a bottle of soda. Little would these fine artists have dreamed once that they would ever have to sing for an apple. And they knew that their wives and children had been gassed the day they arrived.

There was a Jewish troop leader in the factory who treated the prisoners very badly. His name was Schulz, and he arrived with a transport from Yugoslavia. When the prisoners did not work fast enough, or the quality of the work was not satisfactory, he would beat them with a cudgel in order to earn himself a good name with the SS. All the prisoners trembled before him, and that helped him get a soft place with the SS.

One night the prisoners took him out of his bed, gagged him, gave him a good beating, bound his hands, and left him lying in the snow. In the morning he was found unconscious, with several broken ribs. No one disclosed who had done it. Schulz was not sent to the prison ward; he was privileged enough to be taken to the SS hospital. When he was well again he returned to his job and continued to beat up the prisoners, sometimes until blood flowed. Later I learned that on the day we left Auschwitz several prisoners held his head under water until he drowned.

There was also a Jewish foreman who distinguished himself similarly. He was a Polish Jew who wanted to get himself liked by the Germans. The prisoners said that he could be worse than the SS men themselves. One night during the night shift he had beaten up one of his comrades because his work was allegedly not good enough. He then tried to show the worker how much better he could do it himself. But, alas, his hand *got* caught in the machine, and two fingers were cut off immediately. He came to us for treatment. We stopped the bleeding and sent him to the hospital to get sewed up. Later on our prisoner-doctor went to the machine to extract the two fingers. He brought them to the first-aid station. Showing no trace of sympathy for the patient, but smiling, rather, he said, "These fingers will not hit anyone any more. It's bad enough when the Germans beat the poor people, but it is much worse when our own brothers do it."

There was also a Jewish group leader among the women who was a spy. She was a Russian Jewess named Clara, and was in charge of a table of twelve women. The girls did not know that she repeated everything she heard to the SS. We finally found out that she was the girl friend of a detachment leader and enjoyed all kinds of advantages through him. She made a lot of trouble for the girls at her table, when she reported that one of the women had suggested that they work slower so that the Germans would not get so much production. Everyone at the table received twenty-five lashes from the SS. Even our block eldest, Esther, did not know that Clara was a spy, and so was not careful about what she said. Clara soon made sure that the eldest lost her post and was sent to the gas chamber. Esther was a Slovak Jewess. Clara disappeared when we left Auschwitz, and we assumed that she tried to reach the Russians, who were quite near us at the time, for she knew that her own people would have taken revenge on her and killed her.

Still more transports were coming in. Now the people were arriving from the concentration camp at Theresienstadt. The prisoners there were mostly German Jews who had fought for Germany during World War I. Consequently, they had been treated slightly better, for there they did not have any crematories. When Theresienstadt was occupied, they sent the transports to Auschwitz, and the majority of these people were sent to the gas chambers as soon as they arrived. Then followed large transports of Jewish children from Theresienstadt. The mothers had been told that the children would be exchanged for German prisoners of war. So the mothers were quite content, for they thought that their children would be placed in children's homes wherever they were exchanged. Registered nurses accompanied the transport. I met several of my former colleagues from our Breslau hospital when they arrived. All were taken to the crematory. We had been hoping to see these nurses later on in camp, but there was never any trace of them. It was not desirable to have witnesses around who could testify that the promised exchange had meant the Auschwitz crematory. All of them were gassed.

From time to time they brought transports of gypsies from Hungary. These gypsies had sometimes light, and sometimes very dark skin; some of them looked like Negroes. Since there were no colored people in Europe, their appearance caused much speculation, and we thought for a while that the Germans had already conquered America. We were very glad when we learned they were dark-skinned gypsies from Hungary, not colored people from America.

In September, we and several other blocks were transferred from Birkenau to Auschwitz. It was much cleaner there, and each one of us received her own wooden bed, the beds being arranged in triple-berth style. We were even able to use toilets, and began to feel almost like human beings again. No longer did we live in huts or stables, but in military barracks. It was indeed a marked improvement for us, and what was most important was that we no longer had the gas chambers right in front of our eyes, although we could see the smoke from the crematories in the distance.

We were still working in the Union Factory in Auschwitz, but our trip to work was now shorter, for from Birkenau we had had to march more than twelve miles back and forth to the plant.

The air raids grew constantly heavier in Auschwitz, and we feared for our lives, since the factory was the main target in the area. When the sirens sounded we were told to seek shelter under the workbenches. This gave hardly any protection, for if the plant were hit, the ammunition in it would have been sufficient to blow up the whole factory and destroy all of Auschwitz besides.

When the heavy bombers were approaching, everyone in the factory trembled. The foremen and female guards had underground shelters, and I had to accompany them with the first-aid kit. In spite of everything, they were still convinced that their idol, Adolf Hitler, would win the war for them. Sometimes one air raid followed another without pause. The sirens had hardly finished giving the all-clear signal when a new alarm would follow immediately, sometimes before we had even emerged from the shelter. In any case, the alarms gave the prisoners a chance to rest, when they occurred. When the air raids came on dark nights, with not even a star in the sky, sometimes the whole area was brightly illuminated by enemy "Christmas trees." These were special rocket makers that lit up the whole sky, and viewed from below, they closely resembled Christmas trees. When I say "enemy," I mean, of course, Germany's enemies — that is, our friends and liberators, for without America's help Russia would never have been able to win the war, regardless of how valiantly she fought, and we shall be forever grateful to the American soldiers, to whom we owe our very lives.

As we could see and hear, the cremations in Auschwitz continued without interruption. Several prisoners working in the plant decided to try to smuggle some gunpowder out of the factory and into the hands of prisoners working in the crematories. We knew nothing of this plot until we marched into camp one day and learned that one of the crematories had been greatly damaged by an explosion. We were never able to learn whether any of the SS criminals were killed by the blast. In any case, we were very glad to hear about this.

It did not take long before Camp Leader Hessler found out that the explosives originated in our factory. The next morning, just after we had entered the washrooms to clean up after the night shift, the camp leader, accompanied by several huge SS men carrying heavy sticks, walked in. Some of the girls were still undressed. He ordered those who had been working in the powder magazine to stand aside. Then he went into a violent hysterical outburst, screaming and kicking the half-naked girls with his nail-studded boots. We thought he was going to kill them. The other SS men beat them with their cudgels. Soon the girls had hardly any strength left to cry out, and the rest of us thought we were going to get it next. Hessler had those nine girls taken to the bunker, where they were told that they would be sent to the crematory. Then he shouted to us that if he was unsuccessful in locating the culprits, he would send every one of the two thousand of us who had worked in the plant to the gas chambers. He cursed and insulted us and called us all sorts of dirty names. Finally we were allowed to return to our block.

We were unaware that in the meantime he had called in special detectives who were posing as guards in the plant. Before two weeks had gone by, four girls were called into the office, from where they were sent straight to the bunker. With the help of their medieval torture methods, the SS men soon learned everything. The four girls were two Jewish sisters from Poland; my friend and companion Aline Gartner, a Polish Jewess from Upper Silesia whom I had eaten with and slept beside; and a German-Jewish girl who, because he was providing her with extra food, had become the girl friend of the Jewish troop leader Schulz. This girl had often been seen in the powder chamber, where she used to meet Schulz, and because of these rendezvous she had been included with the girls under suspicion and was in great danger of being hanged innocently. The other three girls had worked in the powder magazine.

After a few days the SS were able to pry out that one of the two sisters was involved in the crematory blast, and that Aline Gartner admitted to having passed on some gunpowder to some male prisoners. Since I had been sleeping right next to Aline, I found a tiny letter from her after she had been taken away. It was addressed to her boy friend:

MY DEAR,

I am about to be involved in a most unpleasant affair. Believe me, I am innocent — twice innocent. If one is unlucky in life it would be better not to have been born at all. My life is finished.

Be brave. I pray for your liberation and a happier life for you in the future.

YOUR ALINE

The nine girls who had worked in the powder chamber were released from the bunker. Joyfully we welcomed them back. That afternoon we saw the gallows being erected behind the barracks; that meant death for Aline Gartner and the older of the two Polish sisters. We were glad that this girl had managed to keep her younger sister out of it, who, together with the other girl involved, had been released from the bunker. All of us received a double ration of bread and an extra slice of salami, for this was a holiday. But of course, not for us...

We had to stand at attention, and it had been arranged that we who worked in the Union Factory should stand closest to the gallows. Everything was so quiet that one could have heard a pin drop. Then the two condemned girls appeared under strong guard. They were wearing their regular clothes, except that they did not have coats on. They walked calmly, their faces composed. Having been told to mount chairs under the gallows, an SS man bound their hands behind their backs. My heart beat so rapidly that I had to bite my lips. Camp Leader Hessler read the verdict of death.

Aline was then pulled up on the table, and her last words were: "You'll pay for this! I shall die now, but your turn will come soon." The executioner fixed the noose around her neck, and she was pulled up by the rope.

Now a noose was put around the other girl's neck, who was standing under a second gallows. All she said when they lifted her up on the table was, "I hope all my comrades will get their freedom."

They hung there like two marionettes, turning and rotating in the breeze. It was a horrible sight for us — a memory that I shall never be able to forget as long as I live. The sister of the Polish girl had been left behind in her block, for she had suffered a complete nervous breakdown. Her wild screams could be heard from afar. After fifteen minutes, the gallows ropes were cut and the bodies fell to the ground. They were through suffering now... but how!

We were dismissed and went to line up for the night shift. Marching out, we had to sing our merry songs again. Yet how different did our hearts feel after the tragedy we'd just witnessed. We learned later that two of the male prisoners died the same way that very day.

IV

SINCE I was still working in the emergency ward, I was in frequent contact with the officers and detachment leaders. They were often intoxicated, and if they were in a good mood then, we were able to find out from them how things were going at the battlefronts. The more defeats they suffered, the harder they drank. I remember one of the officers telling me that although things were going badly at the front, they were working on a new and revolutionary weapon, with which they were certain to win the war. As we learned later, the new weapon was to have been the atom bomb, but they were not able to complete this project.

The Russian front was getting closer and closer to Auschwitz, and at times we heard the rumbling of heavy cannons in the distance. Rumors sprang up that they were planning to evacuate the camps of Auschwitz and Birkenau. Every day we watched them taking more and more of the machinery out of the ammunition factory, which, as we were told, was being sent to the interior of Germany. We also saw them round up the cattle, which were loaded into stock cars and taken away. Yes, the Russian army was obviously getting closer and closer, and the Germans were no longer able to hold them back. All of us prisoners were very glad about this, and we felt that the day of our liberation was very near now.

But we asked ourselves what would happen to the patients — would they be shot, or would they be left behind for the Russians? We ourselves would have been very glad if they decided simply to leave us there, too.

On January 4 the order was given to get ready to move. It took a whole day to get everything organized. Hundreds of thousands of prisoners had to be sent out in one night; five camps had to be evacuated. Birkenau was subdivided into Camps A, B, and C; then there was Auschwitz itself; and finally there was the huge camp Buna-Monowitz, where the rubber factories were located. The whole complex went under the name of Auschwitz. It had a capacity of two hundred thousand prisoners, and all these camps were supposed to move out in one night.

To avoid any possibility of a panic, we were organized into columns. A piece of bread which was to sustain us on our journey was put into our hands. It was twelve o'clock at night when our group's turn to leave came.

There was high snow on the ground, which made it even more difficult for us to march in our clumsy clogs. The guards, moreover, were constantly hurrying us on with their cudgels, for the Russians were already close behind us. They were afraid we might be liberated on the way, for now their own lives were in real danger. Most of the guards were riding on horse-drawn wagons. The horses neighed; the heavy cannons roared. We saw great fires in the distance. These filled us with fear, for we could not be sure that they were not leading us toward the front lines. Shots rang out constantly, for whoever could not keep up the pace was shot down by the German guards. There was hardly any rest. In the morning we were allowed to sit down on the snow for about ten minutes. Oh, how we wished to be able to close our eyes for just half an hour! We saw columns and columns of marching prisoners everywhere, but no one knew where we were going.

The third day of marching through high snow came, and we were still living off the piece of bread that we had received when we left camp. The roadside was strewn with the bodies of prisoners from the columns that had gone before us. Some had been shot when they stopped to take care of bodily necessities. To right and left lay the dead, felled as they tried to snatch a moment's rest under a tree, on their backs or their faces. There they lay in their striped prison clothes, in pools of blood that had colored the snow red. Some had had their brains blown out. Most of them had been caught unawares by the Nazi bullets. I could not fathom why I seemed destined to see so much misery... it was just too much...

A totally exhausted man had collapsed by the roadside — I still see him before me — he simply could not go on. One of my comrades gave him a piece of sugar, which he chewed hungrily. We tried to help him up, but before this poor man was able to rise to his feet, one of the SS men knocked him on his back with a kick. Then, with his full strength, he stamped on the man's chest with his nail-studded Prussian cuirassier boots; we could hear ribs cracking. But this was not enough; not until he had stepped on the man's face a few times was the SS man satisfied with his job. Apparently the victim was still breathing, so another guard saved him with a bullet.

Women did not fare any better. I saw a Hungarian Jewess shot down before the eyes of her mother. The mother refused to leave her daughter's body, and since she was near the end of her column she received a bullet too. Thus our column grew smaller and smaller. The farmers had to bring wagons to cart away the dead.

In a large field we were permitted to camp down for a few hours' rest. My wooden shoes were coming apart, so I took a pair from one of the bodies. My feet were red and swollen from the cold.

Another full day and night march followed. Some girls tried to escape by night toward the Russian lines, and we fervently hoped they would make it.

The next night we enjoyed the rare luxury of sleeping in a barn, and we thought we were in heaven just to be able to stretch out our legs. Not only that, but we were able to still our hunger pangs with some turnips foraged from the pigpens. We even managed to snatch from the hogs a few boiled potatoes, and oh, were they delicious! As a matter of fact, that supper tasted so good to me that at the time I wouldn't have exchanged it for the most delectable roast.

Very early the next morning we were awakened to continue our march. The word went around that our destination was Grossrosen. We also learned that at one point, in a small town in upper Silesia, they were planning to load us onto a freight train for the remainder of the trip. But there was still a long way to march until then.

We passed through many small towns and villages. It made us feel good to see normal houses, sidewalks, and streets once again. And we remembered our own freedom in the past, when we too lived like people. Now we would have been well off if they only treated us like animals, for then we would be protected by law against cruelty, as all animals were, and would be provided with food regularly. The SS themselves had sufficient to eat, which they carried on their wagons. The only thing we were getting enough of was fresh air. Our only recourse was to steal some food from the pigpens we passed. Sometimes the farmers caught us in the act, and then they'd come out yelling, "The damn dogs! Stealing turnips from the pigs!" If a guard heard this, she'd shout even louder; "I wish a bomb would drop on these dirty Jews! They're good for nothing! Now they're even stealing from the swine!" Thirsty we were not, for there was plenty of snow, which we had only to scoop up with our cups.

After a long march we were told to line up on a large sports field, where thousands of male and female prisoners had already assembled. We were instructed to line up five in a row and to stand at rigid attention. Then a large number of German military was brought up, and opposite each row of prisoners a German soldier was placed, his rifle aimed at us. We felt that our end had surely come this time. Fearfully we looked at one another, and pressed each other's hands in silent farewell. I could not form a single clear thought. I was virtually paralyzed with fear — fear of the bullet that was about to strike me. My heart beat so hard that not only could I feel it, but could hear it drumming in my ears. I prayed silently, "Almighty God, be Thou with us."

We never learned what had happened, but suddenly a message from the camp commander was delivered, with the order to dismiss us. The German soldiers were called off, and we were allowed to sit on the ground. Quietly I prayed and thanked the good Lord, who had again shown how He watches over us.

In the afternoon we were told to continue our march. Each column marched out by itself. Again, whoever was weak and could not keep up with the rest was shot.

Finally, we reached the freight depot, where the trains were already waiting. It was simply wonderful to be riding and not to have to march any more. Even though we were piled in like sardines, it still beat marching any time. The cars had no tops, and snow and rain fell on us, but since we were sitting so close together we were able to keep one another warm.

During the night several jumped off the train and tried to escape, but anyone who was sighted received a bullet in her back. Some of the girls let themselves down on rope.

When we reached Grossrosen, we were told that there was no room for us, and that the camp itself was in the process of breaking up, since the Russians were by now quite close to this point, too.

Our new destination was to be Ravensbruck in Mecklenburg. It took two days for us to get there, for there were tremendously long military trains that had right of way. Then there were trains carrying evacuated civilians from Silesia, who, were being sent into the interior of the country. Every time we met one of these trains, they always shunted our cars to a siding, our locomotive was disconnected, and we had to wait until they remembered us again.

There were long trains of evacuees from my home town, Breslau, and my heart laughed at the thought that now they themselves had been deprived of their homes. I could tell by the expression on their faces that most of them were bitter and fed up with things, and that it was only fear that prevented them from saying what was on their minds. I would have loved to call across the tracks to them: "Heil, Hitler! This is what you asked for!" Of course, the people themselves were powerless. We heard that whole companies of soldiers had been shot because they had refused to fight any longer, seeing how hopeless the situation was. Anyone with common sense could see that the war was practically over, for the Russian army was steadily advancing in the East, while the American and British divisions were rapidly pushing through in the West. We knew our freedom was very near now… if only we would not be killed at the last moment…

We finally reached the Ravensbruck concentration camp. All of us headed for the lavatories first of all, for there had been no toilets in those freight cars. Those of the girls still owning mess kits had turned them over to others who needed them for this purpose. Afterward, the containers were thrown from the train.

Ravensbruck was a camp of starvation and death. We would have been only too glad to work in order to get some food. Unfortunately, there was neither work nor food available anywhere. We slept in tents, for the camp could not place all the prisoners who were constantly arriving from all over. So we stood at attention again, and the rest of the time we spent just lying around. There was no water, and we simply undressed and washed ourselves with snow, right before the wide-eyed guards, who stared at us, highly surprised that we still had the will power and determination to wash ourselves, and under such rigorous conditions. The cold did not harm us, for our bodies had been well hardened by our experiences.

My girl friend and I still had some saccharin tablets, which now proved invaluable to us. We went outside and scooped up some snow in a cup. This we sweetened with a saccharin tablet, and then beat the mixture until the snow had completely absorbed the sweetener. It really tasted good, and at least our stomachs were getting something to do. But we were not selfish; we shared everything with our companions as well as we could, for everybody's mouth watered at the sight of this delicious concoction.

When the heavy bombers passed over us, we were very happy, for we knew they were our saviors. Passing through Berlin on our way to Ravensbruck, we could see that three quarters of the city had been destroyed, and bleak horror looked out from the ruins. Yet we felt no pity, for we knew that, however late, this was repayment for the horrible deeds of infamy and the torture that had been committed on innocent people.

Because of the many transports that were constantly arriving, and the consequent lack of room, we were pushed together so tightly at night that it was impossible to sit, much less lie. It was simply not possible to get out to the lavatories at night. The only way would have been to climb over the people, and this could not be done either, for one would fall over one person after another. There was only one thing to do: wait till morning, if one could.

On the third day we were told that whoever had a container could line up to receive soup. We were three girl friends, and none of us had a container of any kind except our small drinking cup, which all of us shared. Our stomachs were growling, and our tongues were practically hanging out from hunger. My friend Frieda Hochster, who was always very resourceful, went to look for something suitable we could use. When she returned she was carrying a tin marmalade pail that had previously been used as a chamber pot by some of the girls. The smell emanating from it was not exactly appetizing, but rather than die of starvation we pretended not to notice it, and told one another that it had a terrible smell of tin. We tried to wash the pail with snow as best we could. In this, thank God, we were able to collect our long-awaited warm soup. It tasted delicious to us, pail and all, for this was the first warm soup we had had since we had left Auschwitz.

Now we felt a little stronger again, and our daily conversations centered on what we would do once we had regained our freedom. Of course, the second most important topic was food, and by discussing and dreaming about the good things we would eat in the future, we tried to forget a little the ever-present hunger of right now. There were no gas chambers in Ravensbruck, and the crematory was used only for the normally dead. Once in a while someone was beaten, but it did not bother us too much.

But we were not destined to await our freedom in Ravensbruck. After two weeks there were sent on to Malchow, also in Mecklenburg, and not too far from Berlin. Malchow also had a prisoner-of-war camp, but it was separate from ours.

In Malchow we lived in barracks again. Once again we enjoyed lavatories and washrooms, which were most important for us. We also had straw to sleep on and blankets to cover ourselves with. Every day there was a warm, if watery, soup, and on Sundays we received potatoes, which, however, consisted mostly of thick peelings. If we each managed to get two handfuls, we were more than content. Yet still we felt ourselves growing weaker and weaker, and often when standing at attention we had to pull ourselves together in order not to collapse, for we suffered from spells of dizziness. In general, the women guards were not too bad, and we knitted pullovers or did other handiwork for them. The female camp commander, however, was a witch personified. We trembled every time we saw her march up in her high SS boots, and she never forgot to take her heavy cudgel along, which hurt very much when she struck our emaciated bodies.

We were divided into smaller detachments and assigned to collect brush. Those who volunteered to carry trees received extra rations.

The sun's rays were getting stronger, and we enjoyed the feel of their pleasant warmth. But every night we heard the bombing over Berlin. Sometimes we thought our camp was hit when we heard the loud explosions, and we pulled in our heads. During the air raids, we could clearly see how our camps were marked off in the sky, and I shall be forever grateful to the bombing crews for having been so careful in marking the location of our camps and in making sure they didn't shoot at us, for we did not have shelters of any kind that would have given us protection.

Days went by, and we dreamed of liberation. Toward the end of February new transports were organized again. Now we were sent on to Leipzig. My friends Erika Grossmann and Frieda Hochster and I were together again. Having received a ration of bread to take along, we were loaded into open cars once again. Female guards accompanied the transport.

It was most interesting to see one destroyed city after another. The air raids became heavier and more frequent all the time, and we were in great danger, for the depots were the prime target areas. The sirens howled day and night, and there we were in open cars. Military trains were constantly bombed, and unfortunately some trains carrying prisoners were hit, too, and many of my comrades lost their lives.

On the third day of our transport we reached Magdeburg. German troops were just passing through, and so our train was again put on a siding. There we were left for several hours, and we were all very hungry and tired. At six o'clock in the evening the sirens sounded to warn the German inhabitants of Magdeburg to seek shelter in their air-raid cellars. Dusk was coming on, and there was a bright moon. For us there was nothing to do but stay in our closed-off cars. Our guards disappeared into the nearest air-raid shelter, by the depot.

We looked up at the sky and could not see any airplanes. Neither did we hear anything until suddenly there was a crash, then another and another, enough to tear one's eardrums. We pulled in our heads. The whole sky around us was illuminated as if it were bright daylight. We prayed to God for help. Some of the girls jumped off the train and tried to find protection between the tracks under the cars. A few were hurt when they jumped, suffering arm or leg fractures. Pieces of metal and other objects were flying around and some girls were hit by them.

The air raid lasted about twenty minutes. All of us had pulled our jackets over our heads to protect our faces. I am not exaggerating when I say that two thirds of the Magdeburg depot was destroyed. We heard the fire department and the ambulances arriving, and learned that thousands were wounded or dead. We ourselves were as white as sheets and trembled in agitation. Some girls screamed hysterically, and it was impossible to calm them down. We were no longer cold and hungry. I quietly prayed to God to watch over us and protect us.

All of a sudden the sirens sounded the all-clear signal. People were shouting and crying for their loved ones. Several hours passed before they could clean up the worst spots, and get all the wounded into hospitals. The attack had been directed not only at the Magdeburg depot, but at the most important buildings of the city as well. Leaflets advising the German people to stop fighting were flying around. When our guards returned, they could only shake their heads. They could not understand how it was possible that the depot had been so badly damaged and yet we were for the most part unhurt. What had saved us was our being on a sidetrack, some distance away from the depot proper. We realized that once again most of us had narrowly escaped death.

At two o'clock that morning the locomotive was hooked on again, and our train began to move. On the way we met many other prisoner transports, and we were caught in several other air raids before we reached Leipzig, six days later. There we were divided into groups, and the group to which I had been assigned was sent to Taucha, a suburb of Leipzig.

We had to walk several miles before we reached the camp, which was not very large; it could take only about five thousand prisoners. It was more of a work camp, for it was surrounded by factories. Several of the blocks were occupied by female gypsies.

Upon our arrival, the camp commandant greeted us most cordially and said he hoped we would soon be free. He mentioned that we were one of the few transports that had not been seriously hit by bombs and suffered a large loss of life. He implied that the American troops were quite near, and that he sincerely hoped the Americans would take Leipzig soon so that he could give us up to them. We shouted with joy and kissed and hugged one another, tears in our eyes.

We were instructed what to do during the continuous and long-lasting air raids. We slept in air-raid-shelter cots, three of which were arranged one above the other. If the girls sleeping in the upper berths did not jump out fast enough during an air attack, they would be thrown out of their bunks by the strong vibration caused by the heavy bombers overhead, which made our whole barrack shake.

Food was more regular now. Every day we received some warm soup and a small piece of bread with margarine, and that was enough to keep body and soul together.

Some of the girls were assigned to work in the factories. Others spent the days marching and singing songs. We had ample time to rest after our long and hazardous wanderings. The camp was surrounded only by barbed wire, and thus we were able to talk to the German civilians, although that, of course, was officially forbidden. In Leipzig, several camps had been bombed, and a number of prisoners had been killed. Every morning our first words were: "Are the Americans here?" But we knew the answer to this question as soon as we saw the familiar sight of our guards. Thus we waited from one day to the next.

We heard the rumbling of the heavy cannon coming closer and closer. The girls who had been working in the ammunition factories were no longer allowed to leave the camp, for the foremen and group leaders told them that American troops were but a few miles from Leipzig. They said that possibly we might be freed that very night. In our excitement we could not go to sleep, and waited up for our liberators. The hours passed slowly, and we heard only the heavy bombers overhead again, and more bombing.

As dawn approached, everything had grown quiet. At eight o'clock, the whistle to get up blew, and we were more than disappointed to be still captives of the Germans. It was about mid-March — we didn't know the exact day, for we had neither calendars nor clocks to keep track of the time — when five members of the Leipzig Gestapo visited our camp and went into conference with our camp leader. None of us thought it possible or would have even dreamed that we would once again be sent away. Our camp leader told us to get ready immediately and to line up for the transport. Needless to say, we were more than disappointed, but soon we accepted the idea, for weren't we more used to this wandering than to our daily bread? Besides, we had no choice. But we were hoping to be liberated on the way.

We lined up four in a row, and the Gestapo counted us. We were a transport of five thousand women. Everyone received a little piece of bread and a slice of liverwurst to take along. It was already dark when we left the camp. The air was cool, and we were freezing, for we were not adequately clothed. We walked and walked, and the guards themselves — male and female — did not know what our destination was.

We heard the roaring of the cannon again and saw fires reddening the sky in the distance. We walked through forests and fields with little rest. My shoe soles started to come off, and I did my best to hold them together with string. We were walking around in circles, and passed through the same cities that we had gone through before. Airplanes passed over us, and at night the sky was as bright as daylight, illuminated by the Christmas trees. Dead horses were sprawled out in the fields. At night we slept under the open sky.

After several days, we rested in a large empty field, with German soldiers keeping guard. We were starving, and the soldiers tried to get us something to eat. The place was a little village in Saxony. The farmers were very nice, and brought us raw potatoes on little hand-drawn wagons. Each of us received two potatoes, and we were allowed to build a fire to roast them.

The air raids were frequent, and we would get up and wave to the planes with our kerchiefs. Since they were flying very low, the pilots understood that we were prisoners. We recognized the emblem of the Soviet star. During the air attacks the guards threw themselves on the ground and ordered us to lie on top of them, so that the enemy could not see their uniforms.

Before we continued our march, we each received a handful of raw rice, which we chewed.

One day there was talk of an armistice, and we did not hear any more airplanes. Again some of the girls tried to escape, but whoever was not fast enough was shot, in accordance with the old Nazi principle. I remember a young girl, eighteen years old whom I had known in Auschwitz. She had become exhausted from the long march and had dropped back to the rear of her column. She decided to sit down in a field and rest for a few minutes. A detachment leader who saw her lifted his rifle and shot at her. But she did not die right away. She got up again and waved at us. None of us dared to go to her for we all feared a bullet. Then we watched another guard bury her in the field. Our group was becoming smaller and smaller. Many escaped, but some were shot.

One night we were allowed to sleep in a barn. We'd found a dead horse in a field, and this we divided among us. I received a little piece of lung. My girl friend Erika got a piece of liver. We ate this uncooked, and it was a very good supper indeed. In addition, we'd been able to tear off some rhubarb stalks from a patch in one of the fields. It was a beautiful night, and it felt simply wonderful to be able to stretch one's legs after a good supper, and enjoy a good night's sleep. The next day we felt that we had a little more strength to support us on our march.

My girl friend and I had been playing with the thought of trying to escape at the next-best opportunity. I could feel myself getting gradually weaker, and I knew my strength was beginning to leave me. At times I became quite short of breath. Unfortunately, we had to live through some more air raids. The airplanes flew so low that they could shoot right into the windows of the houses. We saw many dead bodies of people and horses in the fields. They were farmers who had not been able to reach shelter fast enough. Many times there was no time for the sirens to sound the alarm; everything happened too fast.

We had just entered a small village when we were caught in another air raid. The sirens had not given warning. Apparently the Russian pilots took us for German troops, and they tried to shoot at us. Bombs exploded all around us, and we did not know where to find shelter in a hurry. Close by was a dairy, and a few other girls and I ran there and went into the elevator, where some of the workers had also fled. Some of our girls were lying flat in the ditches, others had run to the cemetery, which was opposite the dairy, and still others were hiding in the church. We felt like hunted animals. The raid seemed interminable and I wished I had never been born. When a bomb hit the other end of the dairy, I thought my head must burst from the detonation. All of us in the dairy ran out to the street, and I immediately looked myself over from head to foot to make sure I was all right, for I felt completely confused. Several people had been killed and wounded in the dairy.

After things had calmed down again we were told to line up once more. A large number of our girls was missing, for this had been an excellent chance to escape.

There were several large containers of milk standing outside the dairy. As soon as we discovered them, all of us hurried to fill our cups. Unfortunately, in the mad rush, with everyone trying to dip her cup into the milk at the same time, and those in back pushing to get their share of this unexpected bonanza, two of the containers were knocked over and their precious contents spilled out on the ground. We scooped up as much as we could, and even mixed with dirt the milk tasted delicious, for none of us had tasted a drop of good milk in years.

Then the march continued. We picked and ate the sorrel leaves that grew in the ditches by the side of the road, and they served as our daily bread. Sometimes we found raw potato peelings in our path, which we picked up and cleaned as best we could. Thus we kept alive.

When we heard we would have to cross a river in Saxony by ferry, we had some misgivings, for we feared they might be planning to drown us, which would have been an easy way to be rid of us. We'd heard that some of the transports had been loaded onto river barges, and that in the middle of the river the guards opened a hatch and let the water rush in, to drown all the prisoners in the hold.

Thank God, our transport reached the other shore safely. We marched on again. In a huge sports arena in a Saxon town called Oschatz, there was a meeting of thousands of prisoner groups, about twenty thousand in all. With the permission of the guards, the German people of this town tried to bring us potatoes. But there was not enough for everyone. We lined up in rows, and the supply was exhausted before the second half of the prisoners had received any.

Whether in snow, rain, or sunshine, we usually slept outdoors, and the sky was our roof. Wherever we found a piece of ground covered with grass, we would pick it clean and eat the grass, like hungry cattle in the meadow. More and more we felt that we could live under these conditions for only a matter of days, and we would end up miserably before the end of the war, if it did not come soon. Many of us sat or lay in the meadow, completely exhausted by hunger and cold and weakness. Some were near death. I, too, felt very weak by now, and my girl friend Erika Gross-mann mothered me as well as she could.

We stayed in this meadow for several days, until our guards decided to let us march on in smaller groups, but still under German guard. I had contracted rheumatism in my legs and could hardly walk. Only with difficulty I dragged myself along, and my two girl friends, one on either side, supported me between them. Already we had dropped back to the end of the column, and there was no question but that I would be shot as soon as the guards found out that I couldn't keep up with the others any more. So I made up my mind to try to escape during the coming night, for now I had nothing to lose any more, only something to gain. My friend Erika decided to join me.

V

IT WAS evening when we passed through the town of Grim-ma. We marched past a row of houses. I was highly excited, and my heart beat rapidly, as if it wanted to tear itself out of my breast. I knew it was a game of life or death. My girl friend kept an eye on the guards, to make sure they were not looking at the crucial moment, and I kept my eyes open for a suitable hiding place. We agreed that, should we be discovered upon breaking away, we would give the excuse that we had only wanted to beg for some water. We were approaching the end of the town, when suddenly I called, "Erika, come fast!" We hurriedly entered the back doorway of a house. Then I felt a hand on my neck. I said quickly, "Erika, come on. We won't find any water here," and both of us ran back and rejoined our column. The hand had existed only in my imagination, but I was disappointed that our escape hadn't worked out. Immediately, we started to plan another attempt.

We had marched a little farther when we noticed a tunnel entrance. Our column was proceeding to the right, the tunnel was to the left. I pressed Erika's hand, and she understood what I meant. Carefully, we looked all about us this time, to make sure we were safe. Then we crossed the street fast and disappeared into the mouth of the tunnel. For a moment we paused while we took off our heavy clogs, lest the sound of them betray us as we ran. Then we started for the other end of the tunnel, to wait for the columns to pass. Suddenly we heard footsteps behind us. I scarcely dared look back, but then we both saw, to our immense relief, that it was a gypsy woman who had likewise escaped from the column.

Putting the tunnel behind us, we ran in the opposite direction, toward a little wooded area. Halfway there we met a man who looked at us very suspiciously, whereupon we promptly started to sing a Nazi song. But I am sure we didn't fool him one bit, for our dirty and unkempt appearance obviously marked us as escaped prisoners. In any case, he didn't ask us who we were and where we came from, but we knew that the Gestapo had more than enough spies to supply them with information.

In a ditch we found a piece of blanket, which we saved carefully. We continued to run uphill toward the little forest. My knee joints hurt me terribly, so that I was just barely able to climb the hill. I thought I could walk no farther. Yet I had to keep limping on, though in great pain. I was alternately laughing and crying, and Erika and the gypsy, who had joined us, dragged me up the hill. When we reached the top we sat down close together, to rest a little. I took a deep breath and kissed my faithful friend. There we had our first taste of freedom, for no German sentry was standing behind us, and no longer did we hear the hateful words, "Up! Hurry up! Faster, you dirty sows!" But we knew only too well that we were not yet really free.

Each of us prayed. Then we had our supper, which consisted of a foraged turnip that the gypsy shared with us. Then we lay down close together and tried to sleep. The piece of blanket we had found we placed under our heads, and in no time at all we had fallen into a deep sleep.

Around five o'clock in the morning we were awakened by the chirping and singing of birds. The sun had already risen, for it was now mid-April. I sat up, and a happy smile came over my face. Aloud I said: "Freedom — O Sweet Freedom, how very precious you are! God be with us. Amen."

Before we started out again, we took off our clothes and, as well we could, cleaned them of the lice that plagued us so. My joints still bothered me, but now we were able to proceed at a more leisurely pace. We decided to split up and take turns asking farmers for food. But the gypsy girl soon went her own way, and Erika and I were alone again; which was, of course, much better for us, for without the gypsy we were not nearly so conspicuous, and could easily mingle with the people or pass for ordinary German refugees.

First we picked some green leaves from a near-by field and ate them. Then we went to the nearest farm to ask for food. Since there were large numbers of German evacuees from eastern Germany who had fled from the Russians, we pretended to be two of them. As a result of this deception, we received a lard sandwich at the very first farm we tried. But before we started to eat, we both prayed and gave thanks to God for the first bread that we had received in so long a time, and that we were able to enjoy in freedom.

As we walked along the highway we found two empty tin cans. We picked them up and put them in our pockets. My total possessions now consisted of one lice-infested dress, one jacket, a pair of decrepit shoes, and one tin can. The next treasure we found was some puffed rice, which we collected in our tin cans.

In the next village we passed through we asked for some food at a restaurant. The people felt sorry for us, noting our dirty and poor condition, and asked what we had had to go through with the Russians, for they had heard over the radio that the Russian troops were burning down whole villages, with everything that was alive in them. We told them that we had not experienced anything like that, since we had escaped in time. I had to bite my tongue to keep from telling the terrible things the Germans had done to us. A young waitress, the daughter of the inn's proprietor, said, "We're convinced that our leader Adolf Hitler *must* win the war, for there is something almost godlike about him." My girl friend and I looked at each other, and I thought: "Who knows how much longer we'll have to walk the streets like this?" In any case, we received a warm meal of potatoes and fish, which made us feel much better.

That night we slept in a barn. We also had an opportunity to wash ourselves a little. The lice plagued us horribly, and we longed for a change of clothing. We thought it might be a good idea to ask for work in a private home. We frequently heard the thunder of the cannon and knew that the Russians must be quite near.

At one of the country houses, after we had asked for bread and had talked to the people for a while, Erika offered to sew for them, since she was a professional seamstress. The people accepted her offer as they needed some things for their children.

We asked them for discarded shoes and old dresses that they had no use for any longer. They were nice people, and even asked their neighbors to get together some things for us — two refugees from Silesia and southern Germany.

First of all, we took a bath and burned our old clothes in the cellar, for we were careful not to infest the people's house with the vermin. We washed our hair and cut it as short as possible. We felt as if we were newborn, with the touch of clean clothes against our bodies.

We were given a warm dinner and slept in a real bed, with pillows and blankets. All this seemed so strange to us, at first, that we could not get used to it, and instead of a sandwich with butter and cheese I almost would have preferred a sliced raw potato with a piece of dry bread. These people were interested in hearing about our experience, for they guessed that we might have been former concentration camp prisoners. But we were very guarded in what we told them, for we had no intentions of losing the sweet taste of freedom.

We spent three days with this family, while Erika was sewing clothes for the children. Then we decided to get on the move again, for we didn't want to become too well known to the villagers. We heard radio broadcasts instructing the Germans to get ready to evacuate this area; the Russians were very close by. The people were further advised that should they be caught by surprise, they should offer resistance as best they could. It was even suggested that they throw boiling water — or, if possible, boiling fat — out the windows when the enemy troops marched in.

So we also decided to move on. We kept our tattooed numbers well hidden, sometimes by putting bandages on our arms. We always slept in barns now, and there was enough time to think about our future. I was not able to think clearly, though, for I saw everything dark and gloomy before me. A terrible fear overcame me at times, and I would break out in a cold sweat at the thought of what lay ahead of me. Who would be there to welcome me when I entered the streets of my home town? Would my brother, Siegfried, who was the object of my last shred of hope, have returned home? I could not bear to talk about my home and family; it hurt too much. The word "home" is a big word, and I felt that it did no longer, nor could ever again, exist for me.

In the meantime, we were still far from home, and we still had to fight for our freedom. The German farmers were kind and gave us sufficient to eat. But we took turns getting sick, and we both suffered from terrible digestive disturbances, for our stomachs were no longer used to proper food. We fared much better with sorrel leaves and raw potatoes.

In another village we became acquainted with a schoolteacher. He also must have guessed that we were German Jews, for in the course of our conversation he said, among other things, "Yes, the war cannot end well, if we stop to think what we've done with the Jews. It is a horrible shame for Germany." Similar remarks were made in our presence on several other occasions. It is not true, as the Germans insisted after the war, that they knew nothing of these mass murders. I'll admit there may have been some who did not know about them, but a great many of the people knew, all right. But why should they care, or worry about it, or perhaps even offer resistance? As long as their own necks were safe, there was no need of it bothering them. Incidentally, they were not so badly off during the war, anyway, for they stole enough from all the countries that they conquered.

In one of the next villages we were stopped by the police and asked for our papers. Of course, we could not identify ourselves, and so we said that we had lost everything in an air raid. We were taken to the police station and further interrogated. After they had looked us over from head to foot, one of the policemen said, "They're Jews. Let them go." We thanked them, and left. Our faces were deeply flushed, and fear was written all over them, for we had already pictured ourselves being lined up against a wall, with a handkerchief covering our eyes. Our guardian angel had once more watched over us.

In the meantime, we had learned that about six miles away the white flag had been hoisted on the town hall, and that all German troops had withdrawn from the vicinity. Only certain paths were usable, for many roads were closed, and signs had been put up, reading: "Danger! Off Limits!" The reason for this was that live explosives and land mines lay all about, making the countryside, and specially the roads, unsafe. All the bridges lay wrecked in the water, destroyed by the Germans themselves. But the trees lining the streets were in full bloom, and the sun shone warmly. The beauty of nature filled our hearts.

In a suburb of Oschatz we saw French prisoners of war walking around freely. They told us that we would reach Oschatz in half an hour, and that the white flag had been displayed there. Joyfully we hurried on, and as soon as we reached the outskirts of the town, we saw liberated prisoners everywhere. We knew then that we were out of danger, and that in a very short time we would be really free.

The first Russian soldier we saw was standing guard with his rifle. We approached him and introduced ourselves as former concentration-camp prisoners. The first question he asked was whether we'd had anything to eat, and when we replied in the negative he went with us straightway to a German bakery and ordered them to give us two loaves of bread. Then he went to a butcher and procured a whole salami for us. Next, he gave us two bottles of soda. We were overjoyed.

But we had no time to eat immediately, for first we had to find a place to spend the night. We proceeded to the town hall, where the German local authorities issued us food-ration cards. But there was no room to be had, and they advised us to sleep in the refugee camp.

As we were leaving the town hall we had a joyful reunion with some of our old concentration-camp comrades, who were also on their way to the Burgermeister. Then one of the Russian partisans noticed that my shoes were virtually coming apart, and he gave me then and there a pair of brand-new leather shoes. I changed shoes immediately, and my feet felt much,

much better. I had developed painful blisters from the nails that had worked themselves through the soles of my old shoes.

While we were still standing by the town hall, an elegant car drove up and a Russian officer stepped out. In German, he asked us what we were doing there. We told him who we were, and that we were looking for a room for the night, but had been unsuccessful thus far, since the town was so overcrowded. The officer called over one of the German policemen who worked in the town hall and told him to find a room for us. He said in plain words: "These two girls have spent years in German concentration camps, and they've earned the right to sleep in a room now. I'll check this afternoon whether you've carried out my order."

The German policeman stood at attention and said: "Yes, sir, commander!"

As the officer was getting back into his car, he turned to us and said, "Tonight our troops will enter Oschatz." We could not quite believe this, and thought he might be slightly intoxicated.

The local police department did find a room for us. It was with an old lady who also had two young Ukrainians as boarders. We were given an attic room, but were quite satisfied with it. We thanked the German police for their help. The old lady fixed supper for us, and all of us ate together in her kitchen. Later, we talked for a while, and the two Ukrainian boys told us that they had worked for the Germans in camps, and that they had no intention of returning to their homeland.

We were very tired after all the events of the day, and went to bed early. My girl friend did not feel too well, and had to spend half the night in the bathroom — thanks to the good food, which had been too much for her.

Around two o'clock in the morning I was half awakened by a heavy rumbling noise and the sound of moving vehicles in the street. The noise did not seem to stop. But I slept on.

The next day I got up at seven o'clock. I dressed and went down into the street. And what did I see? I could hardly believe it — tanks, tanks with Russian soldiers on them. I wanted to shout, to call out, but my throat felt tight. I couldn't hurry back fast enough, and I remember that I wished I had wings to get to my friend faster, so I could tell her the good news. I flew up the stairs and hugged Erika with joy. "Erika, get up! We're free!" And I shouted, tears streaming down my face: "Free! *Really* free! We praise Thee, Father in heaven."

Then we walked down the street together. All the Germans had disappeared from the streets. Many of the Russians had long beards, and they didn't look too clean. And although we knew they were our liberators, we were nevertheless a little afraid of them. We stayed close together and at last decided it might be better to return to our room. The Russians threw chocolate to all the prisoners, and we picked up several bars. Prisoners of war and concentration-camp prisoners shouted and sang for joy.

We received permission to go into German stores to pick up some things to wear. We were given several kinds of material, which we brought to our room. Then we took a basket and went out again, this time to try to find something to eat. We entered the abandoned mansion of a department-store owner who, with his family, had fled from the Russians. In the kitchen we found some canned food, salami, and bread that the family had left behind. Many private homes were as empty as this one, their owners having fled, and many of the prisoners entered these houses and abandoned apartments to look for clothing as well as food.

Erika and I did not know at the time that it was not safe to be out, and that it would have been wiser for us to stay home, since the Russian soldiers took all the women they could get, and raped them. They even came into the refugee camp and raped the poor girls there fifteen to twenty times. It was almost impossible for a girl to escape them. All women, whether German or not, whether young or old — not even excepting eighty-year-olds — they took without scruple, making no distinction at all. They got a special kick out of little girls — from eight to thirteen years old. Even old women were raped ten or twenty times. They searched through cellars and attics, even under mattresses, to round up women. Parents had to watch their young children being taken into another room with them, while they could only stand helplessly by. Horrible screams rent the air, but no one could help.

It was extremely fortunate that we did not have to live in the camp, and that we had the young Ukrainians to protect us. When the soldiers came to the house, they'd tell them we were ill — they always spoke Russian to the soldiers — and advise them to leave us alone for their own good.

After four days of this bedlam, the Russian commandant issued a regulation forbidding rape, and threatening with punishment anyone who did not comply with this ruling. Unfortunately, the harm had already been done, and more than half the women in the community had contracted syphilis or gonorrhea. Many of the girls were pregnant. Quite a few of the women and girls had been torn so badly that they could not walk for weeks afterward. Women who had been made pregnant by the Russian soldiers did not have to carry their babies, however, but were accepted in hospitals.

It was on the first of May that the Russians had marched into Oschatz and we were liberated. The war had not ended yet, though, and there was still fighting going on in my home town, Breslau.

But we were free, nevertheless, although our freedom had been dearly paid for. What a wonderful feeling it was not to have to march any more, to walk on sidewalks again, to stand still if we wanted to, to live in a real house, and to breathe clean air again! No longer did we hear the curses and beratings of the SS, and no longer did we have to take the blows of their heavy cudgels.

Every night I dreamed that I was still in Auschwitz. I saw the crematories with their fiery furnaces in my nightmares, and would wake up dripping wet with perspiration and trembling with fear. It usually took me a while to reorient myself in the morning, and to assure myself again where I was. I simply could not believe I was really free.

Our house mother, a very dear old lady, took care of all our needs, so that we were able to go to the park every day. It was May, the most beautiful month of the year; the trees were in full bloom and spring flowers were setting the countryside ablaze with a riot of color. Erika and I would sit on a bench in the park and talk about our trip home and our plans for the future. Colorful birds flew over us singing their songs, or chittering as if they were whispering to us. My heart felt lighter again, and I was anxiously looking forward to receiving some news about my dear brother, whom I still believed alive. The sun's golden rays warmed our hearts, too. There was heavenly peace in the park, and it seemed like paradise to us. I said to my girl friend: "Erika, are we really free, or is all this just a dream?" We could have walked about in the park for hours and hours enjoying the loveliness of nature.

On May 8, 1945, radio broadcasts and newspapers proclaimed the news that the city of Breslau had surrendered and the war with Germany had ended. Church bells were rung all over town.

Erika and I started to get ready for our trip home, but we had to wait for the Russian commandant to give the official release, allowing all prisoners to return to their homes. The Russians were carrying out a search for any members of the SS and other Nazis. Some Nazis took their own lives, in order to escape the hands of the Russian avengers, and were found dead in their apartments by the searching parties. Those who were caught alive were sent to Siberia, we heard.

The German population received some food against their ration cards, but only in very limited quantities. The Russian soldiers took the cattle away from the farmers and slaughtered them for their own use. Sometimes they just tied a cow to a tree that edged the sidewalk and killed the animal then and there. It was not exactly a pretty sight, for they just took an ax and cracked open the animal's head. The blood would run down the street in a little stream, and the Germans had to clean up the mess. We prisoners received the inner organs — the liver, lungs, and so on — and the head. I remember my girl friend lugging home a whole cow's head, one day. Unfortunately, though, we were unable to remove the skin or to clean it. But we had enough canned food with which to sustain ourselves. One day, when we opened two cans labeled "Meat," we found that each contained five hundred German pieces of silver. This was the first money we had had since entering the concentration camp, and we were now able to buy ourselves whatever we would need during our trip home?

Erika made a knapsack for each of us, to carry our few possessions in. She also made some underclothes and blouses for us both.

The first things I packed were a pair of new trousers and some chocolate and cigarettes for my brother. We could not carry very much, and we gave the bedclothes, tablecloths, and dishes we had acquired to the old lady who had taken care of us.

On May 15 a proclamation was made by the Russian administration to the effect that all former prisoners who could identify themselves would be allowed to leave town. We had our tattooed numbers to show, and this was sufficient proof. The thought of finally going home was terribly upsetting to us, and I was gripped by a feeling of nervous anxiety, for I still feared what might await me, although I more or less knew what to expect. My brother Siegfried was my last hope of ever again seeing a member of my family, which had consisted of eight.

We started out early the next morning. Our old house mother kissed us when we said good-by to her, and gave us her best wishes for the future. We intended to cross over to the American side as soon as possible, for we instinctively felt we would be much safer there. At the border we were interrogated by the Russian police, and then, raising the barrier, they handed us over to the American Military Police.

The first town in American-occupied territory was Grimma, in Saxony. There was a large transient camp there for political prisoners and former prisoners of war. Thousands of prisoners had arrived ahead of us, and were enjoying their new-found freedom to the fullest, rejoicing in the almost-forgotten sensation of being able to walk about freely. It was a completely different atmosphere from the one we had known in the Russian-occupied town, and we were mighty glad that we had left there. The American soldiers looked much cleaner and more civilized than the Russians, and I was able to speak to them in English. It was easy to tell the British from the American soldiers by their manners. The Englishmen were much more formal, while the Americans were very friendly right from the start. All of them, however, were most eager to be of help to us.

We registered at the transient camp, in order to be eligible for a place on one of the trains that were being operated especially for prisoners on their way to their homes. After two days we were able to get passage on one that would take us in the direction of Dresden. Most of the prisoners were bound for Belgium and Holland, and we had to leave the train at Chemnitz in order to stay on our route. There was no normal train service, because there were large gaps in the trackage where bombs had done their damage.

So we started to walk again, mile after mile. We hitchhiked rides in passing cars and trucks that were going in our general direction. The very first car that picked us up got involved in an accident. A Polish soldier riding a motorcycle steered right into us, and with such speed that he was seriously injured. We rushed him to the nearest hospital. All five fingers on one hand had to be amputated, for they were hanging only by shreds of skin. In addition, he suffered several fractures. He was taken to the operating room immediately, while we waited, for as eye-witnesses we had to give a report of the accident. After we had explained how it happened, the driver of the car was allowed to proceed on his way.

When we couldn't hitchhike rides, we trudged along from one village to the next, spending the nights in barns. On the way we met many German refugees who had fled from the Russians, and who, now that things had somewhat calmed down, were trying to return to their homes.

The day of parting from my girl friend was approaching, for Erika was trying to get back to Austria and would soon have to go in a different direction. I asked her to come with me, but she said she must get back to Vienna first, and suggested that I go with her. Of course, I had to reject this proposal, for I longed desperately to get home. She looked at me hesitatingly, then told me as gently as possible that away back in Auschwitz she had known that my brother Siegfried was no longer alive, and that he had allegedly been included in the transports to the gas chambers in September, 1944.

Oh, had I been able to fall down dead right there on hearing those dreadful words! I burst into tears, sobbing uncontrollably, and cried but against my family in the despair of my grief. "Why, oh, why have you done this to me?" I asked. "Why have you left me alone in this big and terrifying world? Please, come and take me too. I cannot, I will not, live any more. I've tasted freedom again, and have lived to see Germany lie in ruins, and that is enough."

I sat down on the ground, for I felt drained of all strength and courage. I opened my knapsack and threw away the chocolate, the cigarettes, and the trousers, which had been meant as presents for my brother. Now I didn't need these things any more, and there was no sense in carrying them around on my back any longer...

My girl friend asked me repeatedly to accompany her to Vienna, promising that, once we had been there, she would go to Breslau with me. She tried to comfort me, saying that perhaps what she had told me might not be true, and that I should wait until I reached Breslau before accepting the terrible information for certain. At that moment I saw some women wearing German SS boots passing us on the *Autobahn*. I couldn't bear the sight of those boots. I screamed at the women to remove them at once, and began throwing empty tin cans at them. Since we were not alone on the highway I was not afraid of them, for military vehicles were constantly passing by on the *Autobahn*. The women disappeared in the near-by woods.

Soon after this episode Erika bade me good-by, saying she hoped to come and see me soon in my home town. I had to take the route to Dresden, and in order not to have to wander about in utter loneliness, I attached myself to a group of German refugees who were going in my direction.

From time to time I went to the town hall of the towns we were passing through and requested ration cards so that I could buy myself some food on the way. I did not have to spend the nights in barns any longer, for the mayors of the towns in the American-occupied zone were very decent to us, and always managed to find us rooms in private homes. I also provided the refugee group of which I had become a part with extra food rations by asking the mayors for them.

One mayor told me that I was the first girl prisoner he had seen alive since the liberation. He told me that he had seen hundreds of them lying dead in the road, and would never forget the gruesome sight. He asked me what he could do to help me, and then gave me one hundred German marks to take along. Of course, it need hardly be said that the Nazis had by then been dismissed from their official positions, and that other men had taken their places. The Nazis would never have admitted their terrible deeds, and some of them, when put on trial later on, claimed they had not forced the prisoners into the gas chambers but that they had gone of their own accord, willingly.

The roads were cluttered with refugees, the fields were strewn with dead horses, and the sickening smell of the rotting carcasses was noticeable from afar. Hundreds of huge green flies buzzed overhead along the road. The fields had not been worked, and many farmhouses stood empty. Everything was dirty and unkempt. Of course, we were back in the Russian zone again. What a difference from the Germany we had once known! I can only say that it was what the Germans themselves asked for.

We met a man pushing a small wagon. He was looking for two sacks that had been stolen from him. One had been filled with potatoes, and the other had contained the body of the man's mother, which he had been trying to bring back home to be buried. He was willing to forego the potatoes-all he wanted was to get his dead mother back.

I also met some former concentration-camp inmates who were still wearing their striped uniforms, and we walked along together for a while until they, too, had to turn off on another road.

Walking along on the highway by myself once again, I met an elderly man who was walking with a cane he had made for himself. In a kindly voice he asked me where I was bound and whence I came. I told him that after years of being away I was finally able to go home again, but that I did not know whether I still had a home left. He then told me that he had once owned a restaurant in Dresden, that he had been sent to prison, and that he had been liberated at the end of the war. He had committed a major crime against the Nazis, he explained, when his small grandchildren had beaten a picture of Hitler with a stick, saying, "Give it to him! Give it to him!" A neighbor who happened to see this had reported him to the Gestapo, and he was arrested within half an hour and was later sent to a penitentiary for dangerous criminals in Chemnitz. After walking together for several miles, we were able to board a train that would take us to Dresden. We were still in Russian-occupied Germany.

It was late afternoon when we reached Dresden. The man's family invited me to dinner, and his wife insisted that I spend the night there. For two days I stayed with this family, gathering new strength before continuing my journey.

Dresden had been almost completely destroyed. It was a city of rubble and horror. Innumerable bodies were still lying underneath the ruins. The names of the missing persons had been chalked up on the facades of the burned-out houses or on any other walls that had been left standing. Mothers were looking for their children, and children for their mothers. If some of the missing persons were found alive, the addresses where they could be found would be added to the names on the walls. There was no water, and women and young girls, perspiring in the summer heat, were trying to dig down underneath the rubble to find an underground water supply. One hundred and thirty-five thousand people were killed during the night of the 13th and the morning of the 14th of February — within fourteen hours and fifteen minutes. The people, with the whole city ablaze, were forced out of their shelters by the fire and smoke, and, trying to get some air outside, were burned by the liquid phosphorus that rained down on them from the air, and that shrank the body of an adult to the size of a small child. There was no chance or time to bury the dead, and since the danger of an epidemic was great, the bodies were picked up with pitchforks and piled in the market place, where they were simply burned. Another time, ten thousand were killed in one day.

Before the air-raid attack on Dresden took place, leaflets were dropped by Allied planes asking the people in German to surrender, and to display the white flag in the city. But the Nazis, thickheaded and still blindly adhering to their belief in their dear Adolf, preferred to give their lives as well as have their city reduced to ashes. Little did the SS care, for they knew that if they lost the war their lives would be over anyway, and they did not care about the rest of the population.

Although I felt sorry for the people, I could not resist calling out to them, "Heil, Hitler." I wanted to tell them that they had asked for this, that they had not wanted it any different.

In Dresden I was able to catch a train that would take me to Silesia. It went as far as Liegnitz, which was also under Russian administration.

From there I had to continue my trip on foot. In Liegnitz I met some prisoners who had come from Poland, and in large groups we continued to walk on, spending the nights in barns. But before going to sleep at night we would go to the Russian commandant and ask for a special guard, so that we would be protected from the Russian soldiers, for several times women had been raped right in front of their husbands. A bottle of gin sometimes saved a girl from such an attack.

I soon began to recognize the suburbs of my home town, Breslau, and unrest overcame me again at the sight of this place could awaken so many deeply-buried, painful memories.

A song came to mind, "Weary is the wanderer coming home, to the place where love's happiness he'd once known."

I was completely exhausted, and I sat down by the side of the road and wept. A horse-drawn wagon carrying three Russian soldiers drew up beside me, and one of the soldiers asked me if I wanted a ride into town. I nodded, and they helped me onto the wagon. They took me to the city gate, where I asked them to let me down, to which they complied without demurring.

VI

NOW THAT I was back in my own city, I had no idea where to turn. It was a terrible feeling. My eyes were dry, but in my heart I cried. I had no place to go and no one with whom to share my grief.

Since I knew that there existed in Breslau a Jewish community of mixed marriages, whose members had not been sent to concentration camps, I tried to locate their office address. Standing on the corner of Wall Street I inquired of a passer-by whether he knew of any Jewish families living in that street, or if there was a Jewish community somewhere. He replied that he knew of two such families, and mentioned names that seemed familiar to me.

Shortly thereafter I heard someone call my name from above. The mother of a former hospital colleague of mine, a gentile, had recognized me from her window. She asked me to come upstairs right away, and met me halfway up in welcome. Entering her apartment, I met another concentration-camp comrade there, the husband of another of my former colleagues from the hospital. He had returned from Theresienstadt, and had been waiting for his wife's return from the concentration camp Belsen when he learned that she would not be coming back, that she had died of typhoid fever about four weeks before the end of the war. Our greeting was a warm one, and I immediately asked him who else of our Breslau friends had returned. So far only five had come back — out of ten thousand Breslau Jews — but within the next few days the number increased to thirty-eight.

There was an architect living in the same house who was the brother of the former chief surgeon of our hospital, and who, because of his marriage to a gentile, had been saved from the concentration camp. His brother, Dr. Hadda, was the only one of the hospital staff who had escaped alive from Theresienstadt. He also, as far as I know, lives in the United States now. The architect Hadda told me that he had once received a postcard from my oldest brother, then in Auschwitz, asking him to send some food if it were possible. I was sorry to learn that he had not kept my brother's card, for I would have liked to have had it as a remembrance.

In the meantime, our family friend and dentist, Dr. Schnabel, had learned of my return, and he and his wife wrote to me (the letter was sent through another friend, for there was no mail service as yet), inviting me in warm and kind words to come to stay with them. I accepted the invitation and went there the very same afternoon. They were fine people, and treated me with so much kindness that I really felt at home there. Frau Schnabel told me: "Anything we have shall be yours, too." Right away, she gave me some lingerie, nightclothes, and dresses, although she did not have much to wear herself. After a warm bath and dressed in clean clothes I felt like a different person. Then I went to the nearest drugstore to buy something to get rid of any lice that might possibly still linger in my hair.

I was distressed to see how little was left of the city of Breslau. More than two thirds of the city had been destroyed, and the Schnabel apartment was now in Zimpel, one of the waterfront districts. Not one trolley car was running in the whole city. Such houses as had escaped destruction in the air raids were at the last moment destroyed by the SS bandits themselves, for they did not want to surrender the city with its houses and apartments still intact.

It was on July 5 that I arrived in Breslau, and one could still hear occasional shots ring out in some parts of the city. These fusillades usually marked the discovery of SS partisans who had holed up in the ruins in small groups and were still resisting capture. I saw Russian soldiers close off whole sections of the city and then riddle the already demolished houses with machine-gun fire, where they still suspected an SS holdout.

I went to the Jewish community of mixed marriages and left my address with them, just in case they might receive some news of my brother, for I was still hoping that he was alive and that I would see him again after all.

Days went by but I did not have the courage yet to visit my old home, from which my dear mother and my brothers and sisters had been cruelly ejected and sent to their death in the gas chambers of Auschwitz.

I had given all my documents and valuable papers and photographs to my former superior, Professor Dr. Hirsch Kauffmann, to keep for me until I returned. But I was soon to learn that all these things were lost, too, for Professor Kauffmann and his family had been totally bombed out, and all their possessions had burned to ashes.

I also remembered that my mother had given many of our personal things to some German friends to keep for us. I recalled their address, and went to look up this family. It took me two hours to reach the street, walking on the hot, dusty pavement among the ruins — there was no transportation of any kind — and if it hadn't been for the street sign still standing at the corner I wouldn't have recognized it. The outside walls of the brick buildings were still standing, but they were only empty shells; the interiors were completely burned out. I searched the walls for the new address of my friends, but I was unable to discover their name among the others. A woman in the street was collecting pieces of wood from the debris to burn in her stove. I thought I'd help her, for I noticed a few pieces near where I was standing. I bent down to pull at a piece of wood that was half buried in the rubble. I suddenly unearthed a shoe-clad foot, then a human hand, all five fingers of which were thickly covered with flies, and right next to it a human skull. That was enough. I turned and fled, shivering. I went straight home and decided to drop the idea completely of finding my friends and of ever recovering any of my former things. I now felt that it would be better to try to forget the past and not have anything that would remind me of it.

The Schnabels had a beautiful garden surrounding their house, with flowers, strawberries, and fruit trees. I loved to climb the trees to pick the fresh fruit. I felt free, and that there was nothing I couldn't do. I ran about like a boy enjoying his vacation, for only now was I beginning fully to realize what it meant to be free. My nights were spent in fitful sleep, however, for then my old nightmares about Auschwitz would return, and all the horrible visions reappear before my eyes. Often I woke up screaming, and scared the others out of their sleep, too. About twice every night I had to change my nightgown, which was always dripping wet.

I was still weak, and had little appetite for good food. A potato boiled in its jacket, with salt and margarine, still tasted delicious to me. It was a wonderful feeling to be able to go to the bakery and carry home a whole loaf of bread, freshly baked, with its tantalizing aroma. Usually I could not resist the temptation, and would start to eat it right there in the street, nor did I feel in the least embarrassed about it. It merely took some time for me to adapt myself to living a normal life again; I simply was not used to the basic rules any more. Although I well remembered good manners, as I had been taught them as a child, yet I somehow felt like a schoolgirl again, unsure of herself in an adult society. I think it must have been the intoxicating air of freedom that affected me so, for I had hardly begun to live before it all started, and had lost two and one-half of the best years of my youth.

One of my former colleagues who had been sent to Auschwitz together with my brothers, and who had come back, gave me a detailed account of the fate of my brothers. He told me that he had worked in the Buna works with Sally and Siegfried. Sally had already been gassed in January, 1944, and Siegfried, for whose safety I till then still held a shred of hope, had been sent to the gas chambers in Birkenau in September, 1944. I was unable to ask the man any further questions, for my throat felt tight, and I couldn't bring out a sound. I cried for days and nights, and my eyes were constantly red. I had lost all desire to live, and was harboring the darkest of thoughts.

I finally decided to try to find the house that had once been a happy home for me and my dear family, the home where we had spent so many joyful hours together. When I entered the street my heart was beating wildly, and my eyes were overflowing with tears. All the houses in the block had been completely destroyed. I stood opposite the spot where our house once stood, and from where my mother and my brothers and sisters had started their death march. I prayed quietly, asking God to bestow his grace on them and to let them rest in peace, for they had surely earned it through their suffering. I somehow felt that they were my guardian angels now, who would be with me always and would protect me on my every way. For about twenty minutes I stood there in utter silence, the pictures of my past life and my happy youth, which had abruptly ended in such sadness and grief, coming back to mind vividly.

It became more and more depressing to keep on living in this city where I had spent the days of my childhood, and I began more and more to dwell on my memories. The sun shone warmly in the sky, but I did not feel its golden rays, for I could not help but think that it did not shine for me.

Since formerly I had been a registered nurse at the Jewish Hospital of Breslau, the mayor of Zimpel offered me the position of administrator of the city's old-age nursery home and hospital, for the Nazis had been removed from all their positions. I accepted the job, and soon felt much more satisfied, now that I was constantly busy and had less time to dwell on the past.

There were one hundred and twenty patients in the hospital, among whom was a group of mentally disturbed young girls. They were quite harmless, however. There was an emergency ward, and since there was a severe shortage of doctors, I did most of the work myself, assigning only the most serious cases to our only physician. Quite a few German soldiers came to us with infections on their hands and feet that they had contracted in the war. I took care of all minor incisions myself.

The food supply for the population diminished from week to week. We did not have enough bread or other nourishment for the sick and the aged. I myself went to the Russian commandant to request larger rations for the hospital patients. One of the Polish officials there asked me why I bothered so much about the Germans, and why I didn't just let them die, saying, "You've learned firsthand that they're no good." I told him that I was a nurse, and that I did not want to revenge myself on old and sick people. Besides, I told him, it is written in the Bible: "Recompense no man evil for evil." I did not want to see innocent people punished for what I had suffered, and have them suffer also. Of course, I wouldn't have cared if they had been former Nazis and party members. I had frequent checks made in the hospital, to see if there were any former Nazis among the patients, and if any were found they were given a week in which to leave.

I saw to it that many people who had collapsed in the street were picked up and brought to the hospital if they had no home to go to, often because the Polish officials had thrown them out of their apartments. Some of them living in the ruins, without shelter from wind and rain.

The people living in the American and British zones lived like princes compared to those in the Russian zone. All sorts of diseases and epidemics broke out, and tuberculosis was a major threat. Furthermore, the hospitals were filled with patients suffering from venereal diseases that, for the most part, had been brought in by the Russian army.

The huge green flies swarmed in the streets by the hundreds. The sun burned down on the rubble, so that one could see clouds of dust rising into the air. Farms were deserted; fields had not been worked. Everyone who had a tiny piece of ground surrounding his house planted potatoes and vegetables for his own use. But before a crop could mature, it was often stolen overnight.

Then an order was issued by the Russian administration to draft all women and girls for forced labor. Special kitchens, where they received their meals, were set up for them. All German soldiers had to undergo another careful check, the object being to round up all former Gestapo members and Nazi officials who might still be among them. One former Breslau Gestapo official was found in the cellar of a house occupied by several Jewish families. He had thought he would be safe there, for he had not expected them to search this house. He was sent to the political prison for war criminals, and I am sure that he has received his just deserts.

I was playing with the thought of leaving Breslau and moving over into the American zone, for life in Russian-occupied territory seemed to be without hope for the future. The Polish population in Silesia increased constantly, and there were all sorts of clashes between them and the Russians, who, of course, were the reigning masters.

Through my position at the hospital I had an opportunity to get to know the Russians better. Some of them were well-bred and educated people, but the majority were ignorant and uncivilized. Some of the soldiers, for instance, had never seen a watch in all their lives until they came to Germany. Now they wore from four to six watches on their arms. They delighted in having themselves photographed proudly displaying their treasures, so that they could send the pictures home to be admired by their families. I recall that one Russian, who had five watches, went to a jeweler one day and asked him to exchange his five "broken" watches for one in working order. The jeweler gladly made this exchange, and gave him a good watch. There had been nothing wrong with the five that a little winding wouldn't fix. Another time a Russian soldier accidentally dropped an alarm clock that he had acquired, and when, upon hitting the ground, the alarm went off, the soldier became so frightened that he tried to shoot the monster.

They were easily satisfied when it came to food, but they would give their lives for whisky. Sometimes they didn't care what was in the bottle so long as it contained some kind of alcoholic beverage. Many died from poisoning in this way. I remember one day seeing a woman sitting in a drugstore waiting her turn to have her urine tested. A Russian soldier who saw her holding the small bottle could not resist snatching it from her. The woman shouted. "It's my urine! Give it back!" If only he had understood — but before she had finished saying this he had already gulped down the contents of the bottle. Suddenly, when the bottle was almost empty, he started to spit and cough, and threw the bottle away disgustedly.

But the Russian soldiers loved babies, and often one saw them playing with German children in the street or carrying them around on their backs.

The Jewish community was working on putting together special transports that would take us to the West, but express permission from the Russian commandant was needed to release us. I felt there was nothing to hold me back any more. I no longer had a home or loved ones left, and wandering about had almost become second nature to me.

With some other Jewish friends I visited the Jewish cemetery, where some friends and former acquaintances were buried. Many of our friends had taken their own lives, to forestall being taken to die in the concentration camps. They had done the right thing. They had avoided all this misery and suffering. The sun was shining, birds were singing, and wildflowers were growing on their graves. Oh, how I wished I had a grave of my own loved ones to visit. Instead, I was burdened with the knowledge that their ashes had been cast into the river; even perhaps that their earthly remains had been turned into soap.

Returning home, I sat down and wrote the dates of the birth and death of all members of my family, lest they should ever slip my memory. These birth-and-death dates are the only mementoes that I have of my family.

Eternal shame should remain upon the Third Reich for every street and perhaps every house that has been smeared with blood. The German *Autobahnen*, which Hitler had built, were constructed by prisoners and forced-labor crews. Hundreds of these workers lie buried under these highways, because they fell exhausted and could no longer obey orders.

No, there was nothing that could keep me at home, so I did everything possible to get into the British or the American zone. I resigned from my position, and finally left Breslau aboard the first train that was headed for the American zone.

On this transport I met a concentration-camp comrade who was trying to get back to her home in Hannover. She also was the only surviving member of her family. We became attached to each other, and decided to remain together. She, too, had been liberated by the Russians, and had consequently been raped by them fifteen times. But she had been lucky and had not contracted any disease.

After many detours we finally reached Hannover. We rented two rooms with a German family who treated us very nicely.

My friend Lotte was trying to repossess two houses that had been owned by her murdered parents. I accepted a position as nurse in an UNRRA camp. The UNRRA was supplying former prisoners and displaced people, most of whom were living in camps, with food and medical supplies. We had our own ambulance and doctors. The Joint Distribution Service also helped a lot, and former concentration-camp inmates who were homeless now were sent to the States. These organizations did a lot to speed up emigration procedures, and we are all very grateful to them for helping us in so many ways.

I was able to get in touch with friends and acquaintances who had emigrated before the war. Through a letter that I had printed in a British newspaper, they learned of my return, and in this way were able to obtain my address. Former Breslau residents in many different countries wrote to me for information about relatives who had been taken to concentration camps by the Nazis. The answer I had to give was always the same: "Perished in concentration camp."

In Alem near Hannover, ninety-six urns of former concentration-camp comrades who had lost their lives shortly before the war ended were found. All these urns bore names. After a funeral service attended by all of us former concentration-camp prisoners, the urns were interred in the Jewish cemetery. The mayor of the city, representatives of the German federal police, city police, and other officials of the local government were present, and speeches were made expressing their deep feeling of shame over the events of the recent past. The German police band played a funeral march, and wreaths were placed by delegates of different organizations. The rabbi said a prayer, and then the name of each of the dead was called, and each urn was interred separately. A young girl standing before the urn of her brother was crying pitifully. She was the only survivor in her family. Another of our comrades held the urn of his brother in his hands. He had received permission to take it to Palestine and bury it there. He kept it in his room until his departure.

Several young girls and boys died a few weeks after the war ended. They had tuberculosis, and the disease was so far advanced that there was no chance to save them. Others had to have amputations. One young woman lost all ten toes, another young girl lost her leg below the knee, and many others had to have their toes amputated because they had been frozen and had become gangrenous. The sad thing was that none of these girls had families left who could have made life a little easier for them.

My girl friend Lotte and I lived together like sisters. The easier and more carefree life became for us, the more we longed for our lost loved ones. It was wonderful to be able to sit at a nicely set table and enjoy a good dinner again. But sometimes before we could put the first bite into our mouths, we were reminded of our families; they had been starved, and because they were starving they had been sent to the gas chambers. I felt that every bite must choke me and remain lodged in my throat for ever. Often both of us started to cry and had to leave the table. The picture of my mother appeared in my mind's eye as she looked when she had given me her last slice of bread, as we started on our death march to Auschwitz. I knew that she herself had not eaten any bread for days, that she had given everything to her children. Oh, how I would have loved to have had her at the table with us! If only I could kiss her once more and thank her for all the love she had bestowed on us children! Both Lotte's and my heart were heavy at such times, and we wanted to die. "Please, God, take us to Thee": so went our evening prayers. And God fulfilled this wish for my friend.

One day I was called away from my job. When I returned home, I found Lotte seriously ill in bed. She had suffered a hemorrhage of the lungs. Her normally lovely pink face was as white as a sheet, and she breathed with difficulty. The doctor had been called, and he gave her several intravenous injections.

As soon as Lotte could be moved, we took her to the hospital. All tests showed no damage to her lungs, and the test for tuberculosis was negative. Soon Lotte recovered, it seemed, and two weeks later she was released from the hospital. But after having been home with me for a week, during which time she felt quite well, she had another hemorrhage one morning, also of the lungs. Again she was hospitalized, and again all tests were negative. The doctor ordered three weeks of strict bed rest for her.

After a time she was permitted to be taken to the park in a wheel chair. Her private nurse often brought her down, and Lotte deeply enjoyed the beauties of nature. One day, after the nurse had just brought her back to her room in the hospital, another hemorrhage occurred, and her last words were, "I am dying."

God had answered my friend's prayer. Her dark-blond curls reached to her shoulders, and her face showed a peaceful expression as she lay on her deathbed. Lotte had been released from all sorrow and grief. Now she was together with her loved ones again, which had been her constant wish during her last weeks and months. She was twenty-six years old when we lowered her coffin into the grave.

I was alone once again. Friends and relatives in England and America helped me to speed up my departure. Even before I had received my passport and other papers, I married a concentration-camp comrade, who is also the sole survivor of his family of ten.

VII

IN JUNE, 1947, the two of us reached the shore of America. God has given us four children — three boys and a girl — all of them born in the United States. A new life has started for us. We are happy, and grateful to America, which has given us a new home.

Soon after our first child, Edward, was born, in 1947, I started working at the hospital in Providence. I learned that American hospitals are not much different from those in Europe, and I found that nursing procedures were very similar to those I had been taught. The greatest obstacle I had to overcome was my fear of expressing myself in English. Although I had studied English in school, it was quite another matter to have to speak another language fluently all of a sudden. I was terrified lest someone should laugh at me or make a sarcastic remark about my speech, for I was still very sensitive and nervous about nearly everything.

But it was not long before I found out that all my fears in this respect had no basis. Everybody — the nurses, the doctors, and all the help — was just as kind and understanding as I could have wished for, and I do not remember one instance where someone was ever unfriendly or even ironic toward me. I soon felt very much at home at the hospital, and I began looking forward to going to work every day with happy anticipation.

In April, 1948, I passed my state board examination in Rhode Island. I was absolutely thrilled when the board notified me that I had passed, and again when I received my registered nurse's certificate. I was proud and happy, and thanked God for all his blessings.

My husband, Senek, worked very hard, and for a long time held down two jobs — one during the day and another at night — to make it possible for us to furnish our apartment. Before long we were able to buy all that we needed and wanted. This was a wonderful experience for us, after all the years when we were deprived of even basic necessities, and we counted our blessings every day.

As a nurse I had an opportunity to meet people of every kind of background. Yet in one respect I found them all to be alike: they were all Americans, without hate. When someone asked me where I came from, I'd say that my native country was Germany, but that I was of the Jewish faith.

As soon as I mentioned the word "Jewish," I would feel a sharp pang in my heart, and a moment of fear would come over me, almost as if I were a criminal. The word "Jewish" had left me with a complex, for I knew that, because they were Jewish, my people had to die in the gas chambers of Auschwitz — Jews dying without reason, without court hearing, and without defense. The only answer I could ever find and give was, in short, Nazism: killing and hate.

I did not want to lose my confidence in life, or my heritage. I often talked to myself just to convince myself that I was as good as anybody. "Be proud," I would tell myself. "The Jews were once the chosen people of God. Our great prophet Moses, who received the Ten Commandments from God, and who gave them to the whole world, was a Jew." In my heart I knew that I must be proud of this heritage for which my people had to die.

Again and again I was impressed, during my first few years in this country, by the freedom people enjoyed everywhere — how everyone could worship in his own way, and how the different faiths lived together in harmony. Sometimes I wonder whether the American people really appreciate this great blessing. I don't think they possibly can, for only after one's freedom has first been taken away, does one realize what a wonderful and precious thing it is, and that it should be most cautiously guarded. Here we see families going to worship together, and gathering together around a full table on holidays. This gives the greatest feeling of happiness.

At my family's table there are many places empty. Friends come to visit us, but they, too, have empty tables, and share past experiences with my husband and me. And though none of us ever mentions the subject, all of us know what is in the other's mind. Did it really happen, that horrible nightmare? Yes, a nightmare impossible to forget, which we all shall remember to the end of our days.

There is a wonderful Jewish family holiday. It is the Seder, which is celebrated on the first night of the Passover in commemoration of the Exodus from Egypt. Now, in addition, we can celebrate the freedom from enslavement under the German Nazi Reich.

I still remember the last time we were sitting around the Seder table at home, before we went to Auschwitz. My oldest brother read the Haggada to us, and we were all wishing and hoping that on the next Seder we would again be together in similar peace and happiness...

And I remember the Seder before that, when my dear aunt and uncle, who also perished in Auschwitz, were with us.

But all that is past. We had not expected anything really bad to happen to us, and could not have dreamed of the horrible, inhuman treatment we would have to suffer. It began only a few short months after that last Seder. Not only was our freedom taken away, but the very air was denied my family, when their lives were snuffed out in the gas chambers of Auschwitz. I will always remember our last Seder at home. Our prayers were answered too late; the tyrants had already gotten most of us when liberation fin-ly came.

When the nightmare was over, we celebrated the Feast of Passover at the UNRRA camp, with our comrades who had survived the Nazi slavery. This was a hard and bitter holiday for us, with everyone's family missing; we who had survived were all alone in the world.

In 1952 our second son, Stephen, was born. He, too, has brought us good fortune. Our life became a little easier and more hopeful. We had little time to talk about the past.

In 1956 Ronald followed, our third boy. Although the children were still small, we both kept on working, hand in hand, and we have been rewarded.

I have always enjoyed and loved the nursing profession, and I still love it. I love it because it saved my life in Auschwitz, and because it has helped us to build up a new life for our family in this country. But I love it most of all because it has always given me great personal satisfaction to be of help to the sick and to be able to ease their pain and suffering.

I have always felt very much at home in the hospital. The American doctors and nurses adopted me as one of their own, and when I was still a stranger in this country they gave me their patient understanding and friendship. Thanksgiving Day has a special meaning for me, for I have much to be thankful for since we came to America.

In 1960 our oldest boy, Edward, had his *bar mizvah*. It was a great day, and one of our happiest days since we came to this country.

Then, in 1961, God answered our prayers and fulfilled our most fervent wish, when our little girl, Sharon, was born. We are very, very happy, and I cannot help but feel that with each new life born into our family one of our former loved ones has returned.

We now live happily in a small town where my husband has bought a farm. We deeply enjoy the peace and beauty of the woods, listening to the singing of the birds, and watching the deer when they come to drink in the river.

At night I sometimes look up to the starry heavens, and it seems that even on the darkest night the evening star shines brightly over our house, as if to remind us that God is with us always.

We love this wonderful country and its people. May my story remind them to guard and protect their precious freedom at all times, and to pray for lasting peace and brotherhood in the world.

God bless America.

APPENDIX: SUMMARY OF THE TRIAL OF RUDOLF HOESS

COMMANDANT OF AUSCHWITZ
WARSAW, MARCH 11-APRIL 2, 1947
(Translated from the Polish)

THOSE who passed judgment on Hoess sat in a large room with white walls, unadorned except for the red-and-white Polish national flag behind the judges. The Polish Supreme Court, headed by Chief Justice Eimer, was composed of five robed judges, six jurors and the prosecutors Cyprian and Siewierski. The charge was severe, but the rights of the defense were respected and the attitude toward the witnesses was always correct — unlike in German courts, where witnesses were often treated as if they were defendants.

THE CHARGE. The trial opened March 11,1947, in Warsaw with the reading of the indictment, which contained the following information:

Rudolf Franz-Ferdinand Hoess, son of Franz Xavier and Pauline (nee Speck), born November 25, 1900, in Baden-Baden, married, father of five children, a believer (in God), German citizen, member of the National-Sozialis-tische Deutsche Arbeiterpartei (N.S.D.A.P.) since 1922 (membership card No. 3240), member of the SS since 1923, concentration-camp official at Dachau, beginning in 1934; Sachsenhausen, beginning in 1938; Auschwitz, beginning May 1, 1940; SS Obersturmbannfuhrer sentenced to ten years of forced labor in 1924 by the German Reich for participation in an assassination implementing the decision of a secret court (*Femegericht*)} now in custody in Warsaw; being charged with —

1. Taking part in a criminal organization called N.S.- D.A.P. within the territory of the German Reich from September 1, 1939, to May, 1945, and in the occupied territory of the Polish Republic from May, 1, 1940, until September, 1944. This organization intended to overpower other nations by planning, organizing and executing crimes against peace, war crimes and crimes against humanity; belonging also to the criminal organization known as *Schutzstaffeln* (SS);

2. Having been, from May 1, 1940, until the end of October, 1943, commandant of the Auschwitz concentration camp, which he himself had

founded and enlarged in in the occupied territory of the Republic of Poland; then from December, 1943, to May, 1945, head of the D.I. Office in the Central Office of Economics and Administration of the SS; similarly, having been during June, July and August of 1944 commandant of the SS garrison at Auschwitz and, as such, one of the creators of the Hitler system of torture and liquidation in the special concentration camps and extermination points; having directed the use of this system at Auschwitz against Polish and Jewish civilians, other nationals from German-occupied Europe and Russian prisoners of war:

Hence, by personal action or through subordinates, guilty of the following premeditated crimes:

i. Causing the death of (*a*) 300,000 persons interned in the camp as prisoners and appearing on the registry; (fc) about 4,000,000 persons, mainly Jews, deported to the camp from various European countries with a view to their immediate extermination and without entry in the registry; (c) approximately 12,000 Soviet war prisoners interned in that concentration camp in violation of international law pertaining to prisoners of war; Death was induced by asphyxiation in the gas chambers installed in the camp; by shooting; and, in individual cases, by hanging; by fatal injections of phenol or by medical experiments resulting in death; by systematic starvation, by creating special living conditions, bringing about a high death rate through excessive forced labor as well as through the brutal treatment of prisoners by camp personnel;

ii. Mistreating the prisoners registered in the camp (a) physically — by creating special conditions which caused various afflictions and physical sufferings and aggravated the condition of the sick, in particular by torture during interrogation and by an inhuman system of disciplinary punishment; and (*b*) morally — by insulting, through words and acts, the human dignity of the prisoners, especially the women;

iii. Directing mass pillaging, particularly of jewelry, clothing and other objects of worth taken from people arriving at the camp, especially those sent directly to the gas chambers, or taken from deceased persons in the camp, which action often went along with the profaning of bodies, notably the removing of gold teeth and women's tresses.

During his cross examination, answering a question of the prosecutor as to his role in the gassing of prisoners, Hoess declared: "Whenever the supplies of gas got low, it was necessary to take all possible measures to assure a sufficient quantity of gas..."

Prosecutor. To you, this was like taking care of sufficient supplies of bread or milk.

Hoess. That's why I was there.

Prosecutor. In other words, you were there in order to assure the greatest possible supply of gas so that the greatest possible number of people could be exterminated.

Hoess. Yes, that was an order.

Prosecutor. You admit having carried out that order.

Hoess. Yes.

Prosecutor. Was Auschwitz an extermination camp?

Hoess. An extermination camp in the first place, since 1942.

THE TESTIMONY. After the charge was read, witnesses testified as to what they had seen and to Hoess's personal responsibility in the camp. The witnesses were from Norway, Czechoslovakia, Yugoslavia, Belgium, France, Austria, Italy and several Polish cities. Since the testimony cannot be quoted in full, only the most important sections are summarized here.

The Polish citizen Pajak, who worked in the Political Bureau (Administrative Office) of the camp, informed the court about correspondence between camp authorities and Berlin and stated that the Bureau acted on its own, that Jewish internees who worked in the Bureau were to disappear, that Hoess and Grabner of the SS Political Section signed execution orders. Hoess, in reply to a question from the court, declared: "I never personally signed execution orders." Nevertheless, other witnesses stated that they had seen execution orders signed by Hoess.

In answer to another question from the court, Hoess declared: "I am responsible for everything that happened at Auschwitz. I wish only to rectify various things of which I am being personally accused."

The Polish witness Pawliczek, who arrived at Auschwitz in October, 1940, described a meeting between Himmler, Hoess and Schwartz. Himmler was told that 3,000 of the 12,000 Russian prisoners in the camp were ill. Himmler told Hoess: "There are too many sick ones. What shall we do with them?" And Hoess answered: "Well, we have Birkenau."

Hoess, asked to speak, stated that the description given by the witness was inaccurate. He claimed that the 12,000 Russian war prisoners were in terrible condition upon arrival and that camp conditions had nothing to do with their early deaths. He added that a Breslau physician who went to Birkenau said that the mortality rate of Russian prisoners in the camps was much higher than at Auschwitz. Hoess insisted that the Russian war prisoners were treated no worse than others.

The Polish witness Jan Krakowski pointed out that shortly after Germany began its war against Russia, a group of communist leaders was massacred in a horrible manner on Hoess's order. The first extermination by gas took place in autumn of 1941, the victims being 600 war prisoners and 400 Poles.

Accused of finishing off some internees who had just been executed, Hoess stated: "Executions were carried out by an SS group. The leader had to finish off the wounded. I myself never fired the last shot; besides, the regulations forbade me to shoot at prisoners. I had only the right to be present at executions." This declaration drew grumbling from the public.

H. Langbein, an Austrian anti-Fascist sent to Auschwitz from Dachau in August, 1942, insisted on Hoess's personal responsibility for the executions, since they became less frequent after Hoess had left the camp. However, Hoess returned to Auschwitz for the extermination of the Hungarian Jews.

Langbein declared that at the time of his meeting with Grabner of the SS Political Section, while the latter was imprisoned in Austria, Grabner said: "If Hoess hadn't been there, everything would have been different. Hoess is the devil." Langbein added that Block 11 was, for the most part, for prisoners who were to be shot.

Joseph Cyrankiewicz, Council President of Poland, pointed out that the concentration camps were more than places of internment. They were experiments in mass extermination, in preparation for the liquidation of whole nations, following the prefatory extermination of the Jews. These were not crimes of passion or the acts of individual sadists but, rather, the unfolding of a cold, cruel nihilism attacking all humanity by means of hundreds and thousands of assassins.

The prosecutor asked the witness whether Hoess was merely a tool of German will or really an exceptional personality. The witness replied that Hoess acted like a government robot, yet took personal pleasure in carrying out the general plan of extermination and himself organized an entire series of sadistic actions.

Other witnesses from many nations corroborated evidence of the sudden deportations from occupied countries, of the brutalities of Auschwitz, of unattended illnesses, non-medical experiments…

Louise Alcan, an observer at the Hoess trial, testified at the request of the prosecutor. After speaking of the selection of 200 prisoners from a group of 1,200, she described quarantine conditions, the exhausting and utterly useless work, the "ward" without care or medicine and the methodical organization of the physical and moral destruction of men.

Claudette Bloch, deported from France in June, 1942, with the first women sent to Auschwitz, dwelt on their arrival and their being met by Hoess, who was curious to see Parisian women. She described Himmler's visit in July, 1942, which was aimed at preparing everything for a great extermination at Birkenau. One of the first consequences of that visit was the transfer of women from Auschwitz to Birkenau and the first selections at the second camp. She spoke of the 230 women who were deported to Auschwitz as political undesirables in January, 1943, who arrived singing "The Marseillaise." Only 49 returned.

Jacques Klinger, deported in June, 1942, testified next. Having worked in the *Schreibstube* (camp office), he spoke of the organization of the office, of various labels and special indications, such as RSHA (shipment of Jews to be liquidated) and SB (special treatment), which meant that the individuals had been gassed. He related the murder of Russian war prisoners in numbers difficult to estimate because the numbers assigned to prisoners were removed from the dead, to be used again for the living. Finally, he told how on the day after his arrival he saw Hoess slap a corporal and order him to gather 50 extra bodies for that evening.

Hoess asked the court for permission to speak and denied having hit the corporal. He said: "Even if I were the monster I am pictured here, I would never have done such a thing; it would have been bad for my prestige."

Henri Gorgue, deported on July 6, 1942, traced the history of his group, which was composed largely of Communists and was on arrival received by Hoess. Of 600 men sent to Birkenau, only 17 were alive a few months later. He recalled the selection, the impossible labor, the death of his comrades.

Dr. Lewin, deported with the first group to leave France for Auschwitz, March 27, 1942, recalled the horrible living conditions of Birkenau. The mortality rate was great from the first days. He explained that food rations were not enough for survival. All was run by Hoess. In reply to the Chief Justice's question about sterilization experiments, the witness explained that the experiments were for extermination, not for scientific purposes.

Simon Gutman, also deported March 27, 1942 (at the age of eighteen), related the massacre of his comrades and the total absence of hygiene in the camp. He recalled the *Sonderkommandos* being gassed regularly. He spoke of sterilization and castration experiments performed on his personal friends. He closed with the statement that the defendant, Hoess, had the reputation of being particularly cruel and zealous, and pointed out that of the more than 150,000 persons sent to Auschwitz from France alone, no more than 2,600 returned.

In addition to the testimony of former inmates, an Austrian nurse who had not been interned but had worked at the SS hospital stated that she had been greeted by Hoess's adjutant and told: "You have before you difficult service. Auschwitz is a frightful but necessary work of the Reich. Your inner scars will be terrible; very strong men have collapsed. *The front is child's play compared to Auschwitz.*"

After Stalingrad, orders arrived from Berlin prohibited killing or maltreating prisoners. Only Hitler and Himmler could order the death penalty. But everything continued as before.

Witness Durmayer, Chief of Government Police in Vienna, declared that in interviews with high officials of the camp, he learned that the Hitler regime intended to organize numerous concentration camps in Upper Silesia after the eventual victory of the Third Reich. Life in those camps was to be different; the inmates would die slowly of hunger and fatigue from forced labor. In the camps for less dangerous prisoners there would be comparative liberty. The witness worked in an office that directed the construction of barracks at Auschwitz. He saw that even in 1944, on the crucial eve of the downfall of Germany, new barracks were still being built.

Hoess asked to be heard and explained that he never advised Himmler to expand extermination activities but that, on the contrary, he had tried to temper the zeal of his superiors in this question. He added that the Political Section was not under his but under the Gestapo's orders.

Durmayer said the defendant was trying to pass the blame to his superiors, but that Hoess himself had signed the reports addressed to Himmler. The witness quoted figures to show the part Hoess played in the extermination of Hungarian Jews at Auschwitz.

Durmayer told how the huge flames of the crematorium and the odor of burning flesh made one lose faith in humanity and justice.

Nevertheless, an unflagging solidarity permeated the inmates and probably saved many lives. Who can forget the five heroics souls who were part of the planned camp insurrection designed to foil Hoess's plan to exterminate all the inmates to keep them from liberation by the Russians? The five were betrayed in January, 1945. They were horribly tortured and finally hanged; no one spoke a word.

Who was responsible for the tortures and shootings of Block 11? Hoess more than anyone else. Mass gassings were ordered from Berlin only on the basis of figures proposed to Berlin by Hoess. Hoess did not personally administer torture, but the Political Section of the SS had authority over life and death, and they merely obeyed Hoess's orders. Any prisoner could be labeled dangerous by the Political Section and liquidated on the spot. But the record would say, "Death from natural causes."

Asked whether Hoess mitigated or aggravated camp conditions, Durmayer pointed out that Hoess made things worse and that even the SS men feared him.

Mademoiselle Tencer, Belgian Partisan, arrived at Auschwitz in 1944, after being transported in an animal-drawn cart for a week, during which time the prisoners were deprived of water. At the camp, the many who had died during the trip were removed, the others were "disinfected" and the selections made. Of the women who went to the block from which they were to be taken to the gas chambers, the witness recalled one who had the same name as she. The girl escaped, and they searched all over for her. When an SS man finally found her, he beat and kicked her to death right there.

The witness had been a clerk in the sick section. Sick women were seldom treated at all, and maladies that could normally be cured within a few days wreaked havoc throughout the block. Hygienic conditions were totally absent.

Questioned about sterilization in the camp, the witness said that in the men's camp there was Block 10, specially guarded and fenced with wire, where women were sterilized. Women in the best condition were selected and their ovaries removed; incisions were not allowed to heal, so that the reactions of the internal organs might be observed.

Pregnancy was punished by death in the gas chamber. Those few who did give birth had to kill the baby to avoid mother and child being gassed together.

Witness Albert Blum recounted his arrival at Birkenau in the middle of the night in a shipment of 1,200 persons, who were immediately stripped of all their possessions. The following morning, the roll call showed a surviving group of a few dozen men. He was put in a terrible work gang. After two weeks only 40 of the original 70 men were left. Living conditions were bestial. In Block 9 blood was taken for race studies. Block 21 was for sterilization.

The witness had not known Hoess personally, but stated that conditions improved after Hoess left, and that during the witness's internment there were about 30,000 to 37,000 prisoners at Auschwitz.

Madame G. Kinzelewska remembered still the cries of men, women and children forced into the gas chambers. Commandant Hoess was almost always drunk and in moments of "transport," i.e., extermination shipment, sent for musicians to play gay music for him.

She arrived at Auschwitz on April 5, 1944. Of the 2,000 persons in the shipment, about 150 women and 250 men were put in the camp. Birkenau must have been a center of wealth, since all who arrived were stripped of their possessions, which were then sent to Germany. There was no industry in the camp, just the making of packages of similar clothing, such as shirts, coats, etc., to be sent to Germany.

Giza Weissblum, asked by a judge about the selections, said that all were lined up outside and lists were made. The following day a truck arrived and carried off to the gas chambers those on the list, young and old alike. And other methods were also employed for exterminating people. One was the disinfecting known as "delousing." Prisoners were undressed and their private parts "disinfected." They were made to wait several hours for the shower, then put under a stream of very hot water for two or three minutes, then pushed into a freezing-cold chamber where for five or six hours they had to wait — wet and naked — for their clothes. After every "delousing" many took sick, and many died of pneumonia. The supervisors and the SS men who passed through the waiting room made fun of the prisoners and often struck them.

While the prisoners worked, dogs were often loosed upon them to frighten them.

Mr. Lustbader described his group of 1,850 at the start, tightly crowded into animal-drawn carts; 250 men and 150 women were left when they met again within the camp. In answer to questions, the witness stated that sterilization of men was practiced and was effective; that there was a separate camp of about 3,000 to 4,000 gypsies which was entirely liquidated one night; that prisoners were often beaten and generally maltreated at work; and that selections seemed to be intended to supress resistance, because sometimes strong, healthy men were taken.

THE PROSECUTION'S SUMMATION. Prosecutors Cyprian and Siewierski summed up the case against Hoess.

Cyprian went over the history of Auschwitz, its expansion, its insistence on the utter degradation of human dignity, in addition to the exterminations. After the liberation 500 autopsies had been made; in 476 cases, the conclusions were death from organic exhaustion. He described the looting of corpses, the sadistic treatment of the living. Even Himmler had complained to Hoess that foreign radios were talking too much about Auschwitz's brutalities. Cyprian concluded: "This trial is an episode and a symbol in the fight against Fascism."

Prosecutor Siewierski indicted Hoess directly from the standpoint of reason and morality, since no anger or violence against Hoess could compensate for the evil done by him. "Vengeance is physical violence and easy to execute, but we of the civilized world do not employ the ways of Auschwitz; we treat criminals according to the law. And Hoess not only ordered countless crimes personally but was obviously particularly zealous in his criminal actions against humanity. He was decorated for his particular thoroughness and enthusiasm in the mass extermination of Hungarian Jews, which became known as the Hoess Affair."

Hoess himself had said that it had never crossed his mind to do anything to free himself from the task of carrying out his horrible duties of extermination. Siewierski stated that while Hoess could not deny the defeat of Germany and while "he may now even condemn the concentration camp, in actuality his only criticism of his acts is that they did not achieve their goals." When Hoess learned that camp records had been found he exclaimed, "Sabotage! It is obvious that I was no longer there. The SS had orders to destroy everything." Siewierski concluded that Hoess was coldly sadistic, the most bestial product of Nazism; he demanded the death penalty.

THE DEFENSE. Defense lawyers Ostaszewski and Umbreit defended Hoess. Ostaszewski sought to show that Hoess was an innocent product of the Hitler system from the earliest years of a degenerate Nazi education and that his crimes were but the logical consequence of German Nazism.

After the pleading, Hoess was permitted to speak. He disputed the testimony of certain witnesses. He admitted that many things happened at Auschwitz, but pointed out that his many different duties made it possible for things to be kept from him; that he would have asked many times to be transferred from Auschwitz but Himmler would never have agreed; that he himself neither stole nor killed; that his commands were only the elaboration of the orders he had received.

THE VERDICT. On April 2, 1947, the National Supreme Court read the sentence condemning Rudolf Franz-Ferdinand Hoess to death. The detailed verdict took 64 typewritten pages.

Auschwitz, scene of many hangings, was the stage for another hanging on April 15, 1947. The man who had hanged all the others was himself hanged there.

Made in the
USA
Monee, IL